Walking
on the
Isle of Wight

Patricia Sibley has lived and worked on the Isle of Wight all her adult life. She is the author of several novels, together with many short stories and articles contributed to the BBC and numerous periodicals. Patricia Sibley has also written the highly-acclaimed *Discovering the Isle of Wight, Isle of Wight Villages* and *Discovering the New Forest*. She lives in Brighstone.

Walking
on the
Isle of Wight

PATRICIA SIBLEY

ROBERT HALE · LONDON

© *Patricia Sibley 1988*

First published in Great Britain 1988

Robert Hale Limited
Clerkenwell House
Clerkenwell Green
London EC1R 0HT

British Library Cataloguing in Publication Data

Sibley, Patricia
  Walking on the Isle of Wight.
  1. Walking—England—Isle of Wight—
  Guide-books   2. Isle of Wight—Description
  and travel—Guide-books
  I. Title
  796.5'1'094228   DA670.W6

  ISBN 0-7090-3284-6

Photoset in North Wales by
Derek Doyle & Associates, Mold, Clwyd
Printed in Great Britain by
St Edmundsbury Press, Bury St Edmunds, Suffolk
Bound by Woolnough Bookbinding Limited

Contents

Introduction   9

I Long-Distance Walks   23
  1 The Coastal Path (Part One) from Wootton to Chale, 55m (88km)   23
  2 The Coastal Path (Part Two) from Chale to West Cowes, 30m (48km)   26
  3 The East-West Route: Bembridge to the Needles, 35m (56km)   39
  4 Brighstone to Ventnor circular, 21m (33.6km)   46

II East and North-East Wight   51
  1 Firestone Copse, 1¾m (2.8km)   51
  2 Wootton to Ryde, 3½m (5.6km)   53
  3 Ryde Town Trail, allow 1½ hours   56
  4 Ryde to Seaview, 2½m (4km)   58
  5 Seaview to St Helens, 1½m (2.4km)   59
  6 St Helens circular, 1½m (2.4km)   62
  7 Bembridge to Brading, 3m (4.8km)   63
  8 Nunwell Woods circular, 2m (3.2km)   66
  9 Bembridge to Sandown, 3m (4.8km)   67

III South-East and South   71
  1 Sandown to Newchurch, 3m (4.8km)   71
  2 Knighton circular, 2½m (4km)   74
  3 Sandown to Shanklin circular, 5m (8km)   77
  4 Shanklin Chine, allow 1 hour   79

  5 Shanklin to Bonchurch and St Boniface, 3m (4.8km)   79
  6 Ventnor to Old Park circular, 5m (8km)   84
  7 Ventnor to Niton, 4½m (7.2km)   86
  8 Niton to Castlehaven circular, 2m (3.2km)   88
  9 Blackgang to Chale circular, 4m (6.4km)   90
 10 Blackgang to Niton circular, 4½m (7.2km)   92

IV **Newport and the North**   95
  1 Newport Town Trail, allow 1 hour   95
  2 Newport to Whippingham church, 3m (4.8km)   98
  3 Newport to Marvel Copse circular, 4m (6.4km),
     with an extension to Carisbrooke, 5m (8km)   102
  4 Parkhurst Forest, 1¼m (2km) or 2½m (4km) or
     ramble   104
  5 Cowes Town Trail, allow 1½ hours   105
  6 Robin Hill, allow 2 hours   108

V **Carisbrooke and Central Wight**   111
  1 Carisbrooke to Castle circular, 1m (1.6km)   111
  2 Carisbrooke to Gatcombe, 2½m (4km)   113
  3 Gatcombe to downs circular, 2m (3.2km) with
     detour to fort, 3½m (5.6km)   115
  4 Carisbrooke to Froglands circular, 2½m (4km)   117
  5 Rookley to Chillerton, 1½m (2.4km) with an
     extension to Carisbrooke, 4m (6.4km)   118
  6 Godshill to Appuldurcombe circular, 4m (6.4km)   121
  7 Godshill to Southford and downs circular, 5m
     (8km)   123
  8 Wroxall to Shanklin downs circular, 5m (8km)   125

VI **Brighstone and the South-West**   129
  1 Brighstone to downs circular, 5m (8km)   129
  2 Brighstone to Chale via lanes, 5½m (8.8km)   133
  3 Brighstone to Longstone circular, 4m (6.4km) or
     6m (9.6km)   135
  4 Westover Down and Forest circular, 2½m (4km)   138
  5 Shorwell village manors circular, 2m (3.2km)   140

6 Shorwell to Chillerton, 2m (3.2km)   143
7 Brook to Hamstead, 8½m (13.6km)   144
8 Calbourne village walk, 1½m (2.4km)   150

VII   Freshwater and the North-West   153
1 Freshwater to Yarmouth riverside circular, 4m
   (6.4km), with extension to Compton, 6½m
   (10.4km)   153
2 Afton Park to Freshwater Bay, 1m (1.6km)   157
3 Freshwater Bay to the Needles, foot of the down,
   3½m (5.6km)   158
4 Golden Hill Country Park, allow 2 hours with
   fort   160
5 Newtown and marshes circular, 3m (4.8km)   162
6 Newtown and woods circular, 3m (4.8km)   165

Walks suitable for prams and wheelchairs   169
Index   171

All maps based upon the Ordnance Survey map with the permission of the controller of Her Majesty's Stationery Office. Crown Copyright Reserved.

Introduction

The Isle of Wight is roughly the same size as the New Forest, some seventy-three square miles, yet within that small compass lie bare, windswept downs, the semi-tropical Undercliff (where bananas grow out of doors), pretty villages of thatched cottages and hollyhocks, forts, castles and royal apartments, lonely saltmarsh where only the curlew cries, busy shopping centres, quiet lanes banked with wild flowers, yacht harbours bright with sail and spinnaker, stone barns and rolling farmland, ancient manor houses, modern Hovercraft, wild cliffs and shady bluebell woods – and, above all, walks.

There must be more footpaths per square mile than in any other English county, nearly 500 miles, and all carefully signposted or waymarked and watched over, not to say walked by an enthusiastic Ramblers' Association. Such a rich variety of scenery means that there are walks for everyone from pram-pusher to backpacker eager for a fifty-mile tramp. The following chapters cater for all.

Vectis, to use its old name, did not become an island till long after the last Ice Age, some 10,000 years ago, when a rise in sea-level caused the sea to break through a great range of chalk downs stretching from Dorset eastward. A Solent river, to which the East Yar and River Medina were tributaries, laid down clays to the north of the chalk. So the island broke free, probably when Britain separated from Europe, to become an independent diamond shape, clothed largely with forest, formed of clays and marls with a backbone of hills running

9

east to west and a shorter range in the south. Even the lowlands are folded into gentle hills and valleys by ancient upheavals. Some of the chalk is overlaid with gravels or acid soil; such variety of rock formation partly explains the splendid variety of island scenery and leads also to a wealth of tree and wild flower species.

But before that final separation the first settler, Stone Age man, had moved in from Europe. As the climate improved, bringing a more varied tree cover, Middle Stone Age man was wandering these acres, hunting, fishing and gathering berries, then giving way to bands of more sophisticated invaders, about 3000 BC, the New Stone Age men, who were the first farmers, clearing the trees, growing crops, keeping sheep and cattle and perforce staying in one place. While the walker *may* find shaped flints on the downs from the earlier periods, he cannot fail to come upon the burial grounds or barrows of these neolithic people. Likewise the metal-workers of the next invasion, Bronze Age man, have left many round barrows, including eight on Brook Down. Iron Age man has made less impression – only a few Celtic field systems and one small hill fort, on Chillerton Down.

The Romans came to the island in AD 43. They built at least eight villas and, though no trace of metalled roads has been found, local tradition holds that the very straight road at Rew Street near Gurnard and part of Dark Lane near Carisbrooke were Roman routes. The villa at Brading is the best preserved, discovered in 1879 when a shepherd, unable to hammer in a hurdle post, dug down and discovered a fragment of wall. Today there are walls rising a few feet, and the floors of twelve rooms which formed the west wing of the villa, together with ploughshares, a handmill and the bones of pig and oxen showing that this was even then a farming community, though with central heating, glazed windows and beautiful mosaic floors, sufficiently intact for us to recognize the scenes they portray – Orpheus, for example, playing his lyre to an entranced fox, two birds and a monkey.

Some six centuries later, the islanders were confronted

with Christianity, though, according to the Venerable Bede, it hardly arrived as the gospel of love: 'When Cadwalla took the Isle of Wight in the 7th century which until that time had been wholly given up to the worshiping of idols, he intended to do away with all the natives by fell slaughter ... binding himself by vow that he would give unto the Lord the fourth part thereof.' This quarter was given to Bishop Wilfred, who sent his priest Hildila on a more peaceable mission, traditionally to Brading, though today only Arreton and Freshwater have fragments of Anglo-Saxon architecture.

The coming of the Normans did much to change the landscape. They began the building of the great castle at Carisbrooke, various churches and the abbey at Quarr on the north-east coast, founded by Baldwin de Redvers in 1132. The abbot converted it into a fortress surrounded by a high stone wall with a fortified sea-gate, a refuge for the people of east Wight when French raids were common. The de Redvers family ruled the island for nearly 200 years, almost as a separate kingdom. In the thirteenth century Isabella de Fortibus, last of the line, reigned in queenly manner from Carisbrooke Castle, which she much enlarged.

By this time much of the southern half of the island was being farmed in open fields, with the downs used for pasture, but the poorly drained clay and gravel soils of the north were left under forest. It was said that a squirrel could swing through the trees from Freshwater in the west to Ryde in the east without touching ground – presumably it swam the Medina river! The woods provided fuel, fencing and foraging for pigs. Later the remnant of this vast wood became a royal chase where the king could hunt deer; even today the northern half is far more wooded than the south, which is open to salt-laden south-westerly gales. Small trees which do manage to grow, usually hawthorns, are wind-pruned, leaning to the north-east. (This does not apply to the Undercliff in its peculiarly sheltered position beneath the inner cliff.)

By then many of the roads and footpaths used today had

been laid down as tracks joining one village to another or as drove roads linking downland pastures to farms. One of the oldest is the ridgeway track from Carisbrooke westward, now called the Tennyson Trail and one of the finest walks. Opposite in character are the deep sunken lanes to be found, for example, at Godshill and Gatcombe.

The population was still small, so that when some 450 island knights and their retainers were killed at the Battle of St Aubin in 1488 this was a terrible blow. An Act of Parliament described the place as 'desolate and not inhabited, but occupied with beasts and cattle, so that if hasty remedy be not provided, the Isle cannot long be kept and defended'. In the next century Yarmouth Castle was built and various smaller defences. Today anyone walking the coastal footpath will come constantly upon the remains of defence works from sixteenth-century castles to World War II machine-gun posts.

In Queen Elizabeth's reign, the threat was from Spain. Sir George Carey added the outer defence works around Carisbrooke Castle, huge grass-covered ditches and banks, today a much-loved walk known as 'round the moats', though they were never filled with water. Beacons were lit on the downs to warn of the Armada, sighted in the Channel.

The prosperity of the island in the sixteenth and seventeenth centuries is evident from the number of manor houses built at this time – more than two dozen: the little village of Shorwell, for example, can boast three. With their beautiful weathered stone fronts and spacious grounds, the manors added immeasurably to the interest of the countryside. (Those open to the public will be noted in passing.)

Carisbrooke Castle took its place in national history when King Charles I was imprisoned there by Cromwell after the Civil War – the bowling green was laid out for his entertainment. He was allowed some freedom at first, to visit Arreton Manor and Nunwell House, home of Sir John Oglander who kept a wonderful diary. The entry for 18 November 1647 reads: 'For sweetbreads for his Majesty against his coming hither, £1. For whiting, oysters, prawns, cod, shrimps and woodcocks, 3s. For wine 12s.'

From Carisbrooke the King was sent to Hurst Castle opposite Yarmouth, another of Henry VIII's fortifications and conspicuous from the north-west coast on its long shingle spit.

As the threat of invasion receded, the island continued to prosper, with a flourishing farming economy serving Newport's busy market. Enclosure Acts saw the land divided up into smaller fields, so that it took on the chequer pattern familiar until the mid twentieth century. It is interesting to count the number of tree and shrub species growing in a length of hedge – the more species, the older the hedge, and there are still such ancient boundaries to be found, often on deep banks. In spite of this rising prosperity, there was still dreadful poverty among the labouring classes. Some would be picked up for the army by the recruiting sergeant, here celebrated in island dialect:

> I chanced to be in Nippert Town,
> Twuz on a market day,
> An' auver night t'Rose an' Crown
> I met a zargent gaay.

The sergeant promises the anonymous author 'the king's shilling', glory, renown and a chance to see the world, but he replies,

> 'None o'yer blood an' war vor me –
> I'll baid at hoam, I vow.
> Cuckoo,' zaas I. 'Goo to,' zaay I,
> 'I'll stick to meyaster's plow.'

Many others took to smuggling, the extra money a stark necessity to feed and clothe a family. It was such a way of life in the coastal areas that whole villages were often involved. Gentry, clergy or well-off farmers put up the money for a small boat to sail, usually to Cherbourg, by night, there to buy up silks or tobacco but most often brandy. After the latter had been smuggled ashore at one of the secluded coves in which the southern coast abounds, it was diluted with brown sugar and water. The north coast was involved in 'exporting' brandy to the mainland, where a barrel could be sold for some 700 per cent profit.

Since the smugglers needed to keep the night roads free of intruders, their goings-on led to all sorts of tales of ghosts and apparitions. One device was a 'phantom horse' obtained by daubing horse and rider with phosphorous to make them glow in the dark, and padding the horse's feet with rags so that he trotted in eerie silence. Another was a sinister drummer, similarly daubed, who would sit at a vulnerable crossroads and beat out a slow deep rhythm as for a death march. On one famous occasion a man fled through Niton shouting, 'The dead folk in churchyard be gettin' out o' their graves!' Smugglers nearby, surrounded by the Excise, had hidden themselves in the big table tombs, together with their barrels.

When a large hospital at Ventnor was pulled down, its cellars remained. In this atmospheric setting a visit to the Museum of Smuggling will enrich any coastal walks. Full-size figures demonstrate their dangerous trade from the earliest years of wool-smuggling to the present day.

Ironically the smuggling trade was partly responsible for the rise of Cowes as a shipbuilding town. Smugglers who needed fast boats had started to have them built there; the Excise, who needed even faster boats, went to Cowes too. Nye's Yard was already well known when taken over by Thomas White from Thanet early in the nineteenth century eventually to become famous John Samuel White's, for the success of their Revenue cutters led to contracts for warships. Other yards built yachts: Lord Yarborough of Appul-durcombe, the Wroxall mansion, founded the Yacht Squadron, later to become Royal. The Maritime Museum in Cowes has a fine collection of ship models, many of them from J.S. White, and again a visit will add further interest to walks along the Solent shore, its waters home to every kind of craft from tall ships to rubber dinghies. New Hovercraft take their trials here; in Cowes Week there is a tin bath race!

Till the end of the eighteenth century most of the island's resorts did not exist or, if they did, in only a very small way. Ventnor, for example, was a fishing hamlet with a mill on the seashore, and Freshwater Bay had a pub with a few cottages – but all was to change in the nineteenth century.

Young Princess Victoria found her first taste of freedom on the beach at East Cowes whilst staying at Norris Castle, and fell in love with the island. Later, as Queen, she tried to buy Norris and, unable to do so, bought the nearby Osborne estate where a house was built to the design of Prince Albert and Thomas Cubbitt. As the years passed, the Queen spent more and more time there: after the death of Albert it was her most beloved residence. This had an enormous effect on the island, for the Queen, employed an army of servants, and household purchasing stimulated trade. Hangers-on built mini-Osbornes on the island, especially in the Ryde area, where various large residences can still be seen emulating its towers. Today Osborne House is open to the public, its rooms a feast of Victoriana.

Meanwhile Sandown, Shanklin and Totland were springing up as holiday resorts for lesser mortals. Ventnor, sheltered from the north by the bulk of St Boniface Down, facing south at the entrance to the Undercliff, rapidly made a name in a different way, as a health resort – a large hospital was built there for diseases of the chest. Seaview began to grow with the building of a chain pier where steamers could land visitors direct from the mainland. Large houses were built as summer residences, often behind high stone walls – Seaview regarded itself as a cut above the rest, for those who could not stand the 'noise and gaiety' of Ryde, close by.

When Henry Fielding tried to land at Ryde in 1756 he was amazed to find that, 'Between the sea and the shore there was at low water an impassable gulph of deep mud which could neither be traversed by walking nor swimming so that for near one half of the twenty-four hours, Ryde was inacessible by friend or foe.' Nevertheless, Ryde had a reputation for bracing sea breezes. After its pier was built to cover the 'gulph', Mr Gwilliam, a local poet of doubtful gifts, was moved to write.

> Salubrious Ryde! How often on the Pier
> Have I stood gazing at the atmosphere
> But see! the steamer crowded with its freight
> Comes gliding forward like a barge of state.

This hardly describes the new fast catamarans! But the pier remains, a three-quarter-mile walk right out into the Solent.

One aid to the growth of new resorts was the building of the railways, commencing with the Newport to Cowes line which opened in 1862. Eventually Newport was linked with Freshwater, Ryde, Sandown, Shanklin and Ventnor, a coastal line also linking the last four with a spur to Bembridge. Today only the Ryde to Shanklin line is still working. If only all the old lines could have been taken over as footpaths, there would be even more rambling ways across the island, for they were anything but straight. But once the lines closed and ceased to be maintained, bridges fell into disrepair and had to be taken down; tunnels were declared unsafe; some stretches were sold to farmers with adjacent land and put under plough, so the fine routes from Newport to Freshwater and Newport to Ventnor are lost forever. Quite a few lines can still be walked though, forming some of the routes in this book, and surprisingly others are still being brought into commission. The Newport to Cowes line has recently had its bridges replaced and been opened as a cycle and pedestrian way. The Newport to Ryde line is gradually being restored as far as Wootton, also as a route for walkers and cyclists. This is not included here as it is not yet complete, but stretches of it can be explored from footpaths leading off from the Newport to Wootton road.

The line from Havenstreet to Wootton through Sheepwash and Briddlesford Copses was saved by the Isle of Wight Steam Railway Company, which has several steam locomotives, including *Calbourne*, epitome of puffers, the last engine to go out of service on the island, some rolling-stock and a steam museum. On bank holidays and summer weekends it is possible to ride from Havenstreet to Wootton on a steam train, experiencing that nostalgic chuffing, clanking and smell of soot as it trundles through the bluebells.

There is a long tradition of writers seeking peace and inspiration on the island. One of the earliest, however, had an enforced stay – Shakespeare's godson William Davenant was imprisoned in Cowes Castle in 1650, where he wrote the poem beginning,

> The lark now leaves his wat'ry nest
> And climbing shakes his dewy wings.

Still today the walker hears the lark almost everywhere in the island country, singing as it spirals up over ploughland or downs.

William Wordsworth stayed for a summer month in 1793, visiting Carisbrooke Castle and watching the fleet prepare for war with France:

> I beheld the vessels lie
> A brood of gallant creatures, on the deep:
> I saw them in their nest, a sojourner
> Through a whole month of calm and glassy days
> In that delightful island.

John Keats stayed twice, the first time in Castle Road, Carisbrooke, an area then known as New Village, with a view of the castle from his window. 'I don't think I shall ever see a ruin to surpass Carisbrooke Castle,' he wrote in a letter to his friend Reynolds. 'The keep within is one bower of ivy – a colony of jackdaws has been there for many years. I dare say I have seen many a descendant of some old cawer who peeped through the bars at Charles the First, when he was there in confinement.' Nodgham Lane leading westward out of the village is the beginning of one of the island's finest tracks, the ridgeway over the downs to the Needles. Local tradition has it that Keats was inspired by the view of the castle from Nodgham Lane to write his most famous lines, the opening of 'Endymion':

> A thing of beauty is a joy forever:
> Its loveliness increases; it will never
> Pass into nothingness.

Touring Europe, Henry Longfellow stayed at Hollier's Hotel in the old village of Shanklin: 'I write to you from a lovely little thatch-roofed inn, all covered with ivy and extremely desirable and our windows look down upon the quaintest village you ever saw – one of the loveliest and quietest places in the kingdom.' Holliers is little altered, outside.

The Tennysons came to Farringford in 1853, looked at the wide view of sea and shore and decided they would live there – a decision which actually changed the face of west Wight. Little Freshwater became the cultural centre of England. Darwin, Ruskin, the patriot Garibaldi and Sir Arthur Sullivan joined famous writers of the time in visiting the Poet Laureate. Ordinary visitors flocked to Freshwater in the hope of glimpsing the famous man in his black cloak and wide black hat. Prince Albert dropped in from Osborne. Other visitors, such as the painter G.F. Watts, decided to stay and built houses in the neighbourhood. Guest houses sprang up near the sea in Totland and Colwell, and trade boomed. While grateful for this, the locals remained unimpressed by Lord Alfred, a saying of the time being 'Twice round the island – once round Tennyson's 'at.'

Much of his finest poetry was written at Farringford, but he was a practical man too, building summerhouses, cutting glades in the copse and making paths. His wife, Emily, became rather frail in health, so reflect as you pant up the incline of his down to the old beacon that Tennyson used to wheel her up here in her chair. 'I do not think,' she wrote, 'that on any spot on earth the air can be sweeter or more delicate.'

Another resident was young Algernon Swinburne, at Bonchurch. He would often go over to Northcourt Manor at Shorwell and ride with his cousin Mary Gordon over the downs, chanting his poems at the top of his voice. You can almost hear the galloping hooves in 'The hounds of spring are on winter's traces'. Many years later, an ageing Swinburne met young Alfred Noyes, an up-and-coming poet who settled at Lisle Combe, St Lawrence, in his latter years, enchanted by the cliffs and woods of the Undercliff, laying out a much-loved garden now occasionally open to the public. 'The house faces due South undulating softly to a wide meadow, drinking the full sunlight all the year round and it is so sheltered from the north by the great ramparts of the upper cliff behind it that, when a north wind blows, we only know it by looking at the clouds, or by the unusual stillness of the trees, in which not a leaf will stir.' (The Coastal Footpath runs just below Lisle Combe gardens.)

The twentieth century brought to the island all the vast changes to be seen on the mainland, though fortunately on a smaller scale. Most villages have retained their character in the teeth of all the new housing developments; a few roads are widened for motor traffic but most remain narrow and winding by mainland standards; some downland ploughed during the wars has remained under cultivation, and some hedges have been removed to make fields larger, but not enough to ruin the familiar, homely chequered pattern when seen from the hills above. Modern farming methods have destroyed much ancient pasture with its wealth of wild flowers and grasses but these still exist on the steep, unimproved flanks of the downs.

It is fashionable to decry forestry plantations of conifers, with their straight lines, dim aisles and unproductive forest floor – those planted by the Forestry Commission have encroached on downland and some northern coast; yet they do add to the island's comparatively small acreage of woodland and have been gratefully colonized by the red squirrel, badger and flocks of tits, among others. Today the Commission plants with more concern for landscape: Brighstone Forest, still young, will one day be a magnificent beech wood clothing the northern slopes, and already it provides miles of peaceful walking, away from the summer hordes.

For there is a great invasion of visitors every summer: the whole island economy depends upon it. Many of the large houses built when Queen Victoria at Osborne made it so fashionable are now hotels. Of the thousands who throng Ryde, Sandown, Shanklin, Ventnor and various holiday camps, the majority come from towns; they enjoy getting out in the country with its many reassuring signposts, but only the real walkers get very far: many footpaths are well used for about half a mile, much less so after that. So if at the height of August a path seems rather crowded, walk on and quite soon you will probably have it to yourself.

One twentieth-century development of enormous service to the walker is the bus service which spreads out in a spider's web centred on Newport and covers the whole island. Even small rural communities well off the main roads, such as Newtown and Atherfield, are served by a post bus. The time-table is a booklet stuffed with information on places of interest, opening times and maps; there is no easier place to explore for the walker without a car. For those who do bring their own transport, buses are still very useful, since not all walks are circular. Anyone who has walked the fine down ridge twelve miles from Carisbrooke to the Needles [pp.42-6] may prefer to drop down into Alum Bay for a bus rather than turn round to walk back again.

Compared with most mainland counties, villages are closer together, and most of them have a pub. Very many of these have outdoor tables and gardens where children are welcome, and provide a variety of food from sandwiches to a three-course meal.

You are comfortingly close to a bus home then, or a good meal, yet you can walk for hours even in high summer without meeting a soul or glimpsing a red roof.

Walking conditions are good on the whole – the word 'rough' often means trampled by cattle or stony. Nowhere are there conditions as truly 'rough' as, say Ingleborough or on Dartmoor scree, so real walking-boots are not necessary. What the walker does need, often in summer as well as winter, is good waterproof footwear, such as short wellingtons.

Our countryside treasures are closely watched and guarded by the Hampshire and Isle of Wight Naturalists Trust and by the Isle of Wight Natural History Society. Apart from the red squirrel, now extinct in mainland Hampshire, two particular rarities are the Glanville fritillary, a butterfly which breeds along the southern cliffs, and wood calamint, a plant whose only known site in Britain is beside a chalky track leading up to the downs. The Nature Conservancy Council had designated many Sites of Special Scientific Interest protecting such habitats as the wetlands at Newtown and the flora of Compton Down. Various orchids flourish still – readers of this book will be too fond of the countryside to pick them and prevent their seeding.

Several exhibitions which add interest to walking are noted in the course of the following chapters. One which covers the whole island is 'Local Look', staged each year in Brook by the Natural History Society for the month of August, with a different theme each year. A recent Local Look was called Finding Out, which investigated various ways of enjoying fieldwork on the island for both professional and amateur naturalists, including maps to show the most likely places to see red squirrels, night-flying moths and dinosaur bones. One photograph which drew all eyes was of a dormouse wearing a collar – it bore a minute radio transmitter, part of

National Dormouse Project. Other exhibits showed various kinds of bat, favourite badger habitats, and how to estimate the age of a hedge and recognize a Glanville fritillary.

A stand of particular interest to the walker showed views of the Tennyson Trail, from Carisbrooke to the Needles, taken from the air to show the wealth of archaeological remains along this chalk ridge, including a recently discovered neolithic enclosure. Another panel pictured the amazing variety of wild flowers to be found in a patch of chalk down one metre square over three months. Others gave a history of windows and doors in farmhouses and cottages, rook, heron and ringed plover surveys, mosses, fungi, rocks and rockpools. Local Look is rather like a wine-tasting, a brief glimpse of all the natural history to be enjoyed at leisure. There are also many leaflets and nature-trail guides on sale, brought out by the local Natural History Society.

One panel dealt with weather. Even the most up-to-date computers cannot deal with the complexities of Isle of Wight weather, it is so local. Channel fog often drifts in over the south-west while the rest is bathed in sunshine; Newport may swelter in humid seventies while a cool breeze blows along the coast. The walker can very often take advantage of these variable conditions: since the treeless south-west coast and downs are exposed to the prevailing south-westerly winds, this fine walking country is best reserved for calmer days, but central Wight is always more sheltered.

I   Long-Distance Walks

In 1973 the Isle of Wight County Council announced a new series of long-distance paths, waymarked with red paint and each accompanied by a leaflet. These were the Coastal Path (divided into four sections) and the Shepherd's, Nunwell, Worsley, Hamstead, Stenbury, Bembridge and Tennyson Trails. To these have been added the Freshwater Way and, most recently, the Downland Way. All except the last are marked and named on the Ordnance Survey Map 'Solent and the Isle of Wight', sheet 196 in their Landranger series, on the useful scale of 1¼ inches to a mile. On the ground these are marked by signposts where necessary. Some of the old red-painted waymarks remain but were found to need much upkeep; most have been replaced by yellow and blue tin arrows.

Walk 1: The Coastal Path (Part One) from Wootton to Chale
Distance: 55 miles (88 kilometres)
Map: *see* pp. 24-5

The entire coastal path, except the dull road-stretch from East Cowes to Wootton, is described in this book in short stretches from Wootton round to Chale, where it is frequently broken by towns or villages, on pp.53-92, and in one stretch from Chale to West Cowes, on pp.26-38. The Hamstead Trail is described on pp.144-9. Part of the Worsley, Stenbury and

Chapter 1

WALK 1 : The Coastal Path (Part One) from Wootton to Chale
WALK 2 : The Coastal Path (Part Two) from Chale to West Cowes

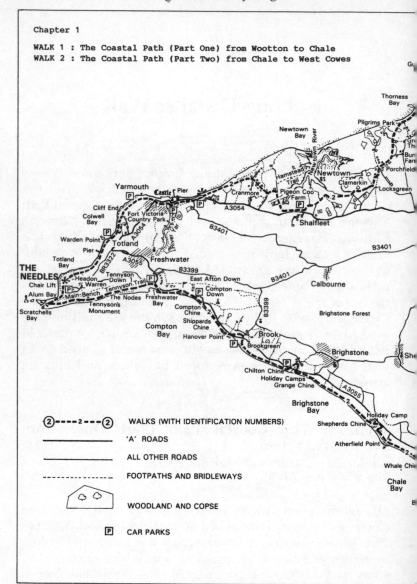

②----2----②	WALKS (WITH IDENTIFICATION NUMBERS)
———————	'A' ROADS
———————	ALL OTHER ROADS
- - - - - - -	FOOTPATHS AND BRIDLEWAYS
⌂	WOODLAND AND COPSE
P	CAR PARKS

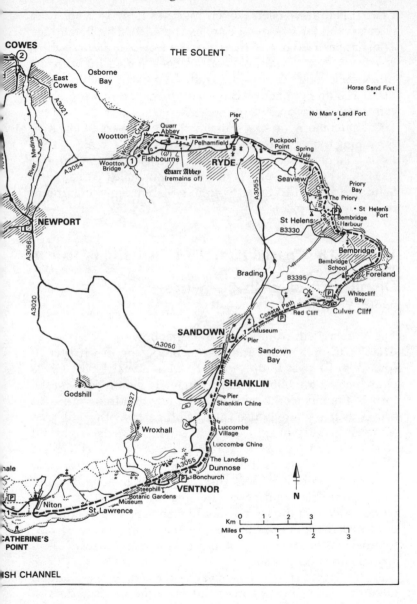

Coastal Path have been woven together to make a splendid circular walk of twenty-one miles (pp.46-9). The Bembridge Trail has been left out, in favour of the Downland Way, which covers the same ground. This has been joined up with the fifteen-mile-long Tennyson Trail, bypassing Newport, to make a route right across the island from east to west, about thirty-two miles (pp.39-46).

Considerations of space mean that only part of the two remaining trails are covered. Shepherd's Trail, ten miles, runs from Shepherd's Chine, near Chale, to Carisbrooke (p.113). The Nunwell Trail, also ten miles runs from Sandown Station to Ryde St John's Station, enabling one to return by train (p.26).

Walk 2: The Coastal Path (Part Two) from Chale to West Cowes
Distance: 30 miles (48 kilometres)
Map: *see* pp.24-5

The Coastal Path from Wootton to Sandown is described in Chapter II (pp.53-69), Sandown to Blackgang in Chapter III (pp.77-94).To pick it up, we set out westward past Chale church along the Military Road originally built to join coastal forts in the nineteenth century. In a few hundred yards this brings us to a white house called Cliff Farm, with a stile and signpost just beyond it. The path follows a hedge right out across a broad pasture to rough grass along the cliff edge. From here you can see the whole of the south-west coast laid out ahead, red-brown cliffs curving into Brighstone Bay, out to Hanover Point and soon after rearing higher, turning to white chalk with the long wall of Freshwater cliffs ending in the Needles rocks – a splendid, exhilarating stretch of coast for the walker, though not quite as straightforward as it appears from this distance.

Soon it is broken by two small chines, Walpen and Ladder, mere bare-sided ravines now but once the headquarters of

Chale's fishing. Robert Wheeler's log for a June day in 1790 reads: 'In the morning we caught one thousand one hundred mackerel and a large turbot. There was a large quantity of mackerel seen to play in the evening.'

The path continues along the cliff edge, skirting a vast field, till forced inland by Whale Chine, which has to be crossed by the roadbridge; after a car-park, a signpost points out across the next field to the cliff edge again, but Whale Chine is worth a detour, a miniature Arizona canyon with almost sheer sides of bare rock, so deep and narrow that it is always cool and shadowy at the bottom even in high summer. Dozens of steps, narrow paths and a bridge or two at last lead out onto the wild shore, steep and shingly, with a sinister undertow always to be heard growling among the rocks.

Back along the cliff edge we presently pass close to a neat row of coastguard cottages. Below them stretch the rocks of Atherfield Reef. In January 1892 passengers on the steamship *Eider* were enjoying a concert when she ran aground here in thick fog. Working all night, the three local lifeboats brought ashore almost 400 people.

The next chine, Shepherd's, means another detour back to the road, over a bridge and then out onto the cliffs again, skirting Atherfield holiday camp, but this is the last chine for two miles. The cliff climbs up to Barnes High. (There used to be Barnes Chine too, but the sea has eroded it all away.) A long cliff-top stretch with fine views inland of the downs brings us to the vicinity of Brighstone. Grange Chine is wide and green – no need to walk round it: the path goes quite steeply down its flank to the beach, crossing a stream by a wooden footbridge, and continues up the other side, past some caravans back onto the cliff top.

You can detour to Brighstone by walking up through the chine, crossing the road and taking a path through fields, signposted just to the left of the turn-off to the village.

During the Napoleonic Wars, Grange Chine held a barracks full of soldiers ready to repel a French invasion, and later the lifeboat house, but both have been washed away.

The cliff path leads over several stiles across the seaward side of Brighstone holiday camp. The shore below is less threatening now, with acres of sand and pink-brown rock ledges when the tide is out, good for prawning.

At Chilton Chine we have to go inland again, past a holiday centre, then turn back down a green path skirting the cleft to the cliffs, bright in summer with sea-pink, sea-carrot and yellow kidney vetch. Further along, large stretches of cliff edge have fallen, sometimes halfway down, sometimes only a few feet, wet ledges where orchids grow and frogs breed in shallow ponds.

Brook village straggles from the downs to the sea, its last houses right out on the cliff – the very last, now resembling a garage was the home of the Brook lifeboat. Here we turn inland along the gravel track in front of the cottages back to the Military Road. A turning opposite leads up through the village to the downs, or in a few yards to Hanover House restaurant. A few yards along, the coast road turn into the car-park, and the path continues over a stile, not far above the beach now, for the cliffs are low and crumbling, perilously near the road and eating back every year towards it. Below, just out in the sea, a small tower marks the reef off Hanover Point where cormorants often perch, hanging out their black wings to dry. The reef is very special, the remains of an ancient pine forest.

Crossing the headland, we reach a car-park, a stile on the other side and the last stretch of low cliffs, which dip down to a long series of steps and catwalks giving access to the beach, here flat, sandy and safe for bathing.

Ahead, the cliff rears up, changing nature entirely, to sheer chalk plunging to the sea. The path climbs up and along the edge, an uncluttered mile and a half of green turf and dramatic coastal scenery, but if you do not like heights, avoid it by walking along the coast road close by or taking to the downs just across it. The path eventually leads down into Freshwater Bay, a tiny, almost circular breach in the high cliffs with one or two fishing boats in the harbour, a few hotels and shops. Walk along a high sea wall to the road and past the Albion Hotel, where a tarmac lane leads off to the left. This is actually the old road to Fort Redoubt on the cliff top, now a café with a breathtaking view down into Freshwater Bay and beyond. A deep, narrow moat separates it from the land; a bridge and tunnel through the massive outer wall form the entrance.

Where a stile marks the foot of Tennyson Down, it is possible, with care, to stand on the edge and look down onto the rocky shore below and the cliff face where samphire and sea-pink find root on small ledges. The samphire used to be gathered by men dangling on ropes; then it was pickled and sent to London in barrels. Over the stile a steep climb leads away from the cliff edge and up onto the summit ridge towards a granite cross on the down's height, 480 feet, a memorial to Alfred, Lord Tennyson, who loved to walk up here from his home at Farringford.

These three miles to the Needles must be one of the finest walks on the island, the great green headland narrowing all the time, sloping down on one side to the narrow Solent and distant views of the New Forest and western coast right down into Dorset, while to the south are great cliffs with gulls eddying and crying far below, where waves boom and echo through deep caves.

The turf levels out into a ridge walk, with a real top-of-the-world feeling, till it begins to descend toward the Needles. For many years this part was out of bounds to walkers, as it was used as a testing site for Black Knight rockets. Now it has been cleared up and opened to the public by the National Trust, though you can still trace old bunkers and buildings in the bumpy terrain. The National Trust also took over the row of old coastguard cottages below; they are now done up and let to holiday-makers.

The land grows very narrow now, a mere wedge of turf. You can look down and back into Scratchell's Bay, where the strata are so tilted that the white cliff is striped up and down with bands of dark flint, above gaping cave mouths, while ahead lie the famous Needles and the red-and-white striped lighthouse. Even so, this is not the very tip of the island – that is taken up by a fort (open in summer) reached under an archway bearing the sign 'Needles Battery, 1862' and across a drawbridge. Inside the fort, a circular staircase leads down to a tunnel through the solid chalk which comes out on a precipitous ledge with the Needles right below. You really cannot take a further step westward!

Continuing on the Coastal Path from the Needles, we take a narrow tarmac road downhill from the fort gate, with a view down into Alum Bay and another spectacular change of cliff scenery, for while we are still on chalk, the bay within the right angle ahead glows with ochre and orange, deep red, pale cream and every shade of tawny brown – Alum Bay is famous for its coloured sands, the colours growing clearer as we come down off the heights. In the last century the sands were used to 'paint' local views; today they fill glass souvenirs. Our narrow road meets the main road at a hotel entrance. Here you can cross over and descend steps to a wooded chine leading to the beach or take the road for a few hundred yards before turning up a stony track to continue the Coastal Path.

The path leads up over the shoulder of Headon Hill or Warren, past ruins of yet another fort, up onto a gravelly ridge patched with heather and gorse, in contrast to the smooth chalk turf of Tennyson Down, which rises like a great wall to the south. Not only rabbits live in this warren: some holes have been taken over by sand martins. To the north, land falls away in hummocks to the Solent. Various paths, all rather stony, criss-cross the hill, but it is not possible to lose your way if you keep roughly along the crest of the ridge from which the red roofs of Totland soon come into view below, bowered in trees.

We follow the path downhill, suddenly coming upon an isolated house, and, following a chestnut fence, come to an enclosed pathway to a kissing-gate onto a gravel lane, with a view right across to Brighstone Forest, while two forts demand attention in the foreground: Fort Albert jutting out into the sea, and Golden Hill, white and striking just inland.

At the road junction we turn downhill through the outskirts of Totland. (Halfway down, a steep track with iron pillars across the entrance would take you down onto the shore.) We continue on down till the Turf Walk opens out beside the road, a pleasant cliff-top expanse of grass, a kind of grandstand for viewing the Solent, with plenty of seats. At the far end a road leads up to Totland village, the Seaview of west Wight, most of its large houses built as summer residences for visitors from the mainland. Many were planned by the same architect, who liked the russet tiles, little turrets and fancy gables which still lend Totland its character.

To walk on to Colwell, cross a footbridge over the road below, continue along a short stretch of cliff, turn inland for a few yards, then mount some steps signposted to Colwell and keep along a well-defined field path. This might be a good idea if there is a very high tide, but it is more interesting to walk under the footbridge down into Totland Bay and take the sea wall.

Where the road ends stands a small pier where steamers used to call to unload summer visitors. In summer there is a café, restaurant, canoes. We follow the wide sea wall eastward, crumbling yellow cliffs on one side, patched with tamarisk and tree mallow, and on the other a narrow sand and shingle beach broken up by wooden breakwaters which do not prevent waves slapping the wall and sending up clouds of spray at spring tides. Across the Solent, right opposite, Hurst Castle juts out into the sea on its long pebble spit: here Charles I was kept prisoner after he was taken from Carisbrooke. The wall leads out to Warden Point, where a reef shows black rocks, a good place to see gulls and terns fishing. Pause here and look back, for there's a fine view of the Needles and their lighthouse, looking surprisingly tall and close from water-level.

Round the point, we are looking into Colwell Bay, in character much like Totland, though without a pier. The slipway was used to unload heavy guns for the many forts in west Wight. Here also are small cafés and beach huts. (One could make a round walk from Totland by taking the field path to Colwell, which comes out right by the shore, and returning along the sea wall.)

We carry on round the bay still on the sea wall, heading for Fort Albert, which stands four-square in the sea off the next headland. Once an experimental station for torpedoes, it has recently been converted into luxury flats. However, the sea wall does not reach right round the bay, and a steep ramp climbs the cliff to skirt an estate of holiday bungalows. At a T-junction turn left onto a narrow green footpath for a short stretch. Coming out among bungalows again, turn right into Monks Lane for a few hundred yards, then, following a signpost to Fort Victoria, turn toward the cliff edge again. Here you can see the track ahead, curving downhill, then up again towards a small square turret, part of Cliff End. Past the last bungalows we skirt the remains of this small fort, never a great success as its walls cracked every time a gun was fired! Nevertheless, we owe to it the delightful stretch ahead. The army once built a cobbled road to join Cliff End to Fort Victoria along the low cliff top. Over the years grass has grown across the stones, and old woods overhang it, making it a thoroughfare for rabbits rather than guns, and a shady walk for a hot summer's day. Here and there cliff falls make a break in the seaward woods, providing a fine view of the western Solent and Hurst Castle opposite.

A footpath and steps descend the cliff through the woods, coming out on a vast green lawn with the shore on one side and Fort Victoria's brick ramparts on the other. On its north side the huge wall is pierced by ten circular gun ports like immense rabbit-holes. There is a café and sea aquarium, and steps up onto the roof. Because shipping comes close inshore here to avoid Hurst Spit, it is a popular vantage-point for watching the start of the Fastnet and Powerboat races, and always a good picnic spot, with its tables and benches right by the sea.

We continue along a narrow road from the car-park, passing an old jetty and a boatyard and, where the road swings inland, carry straight on down a narrow path through the sycamores to a broad sea wall with a view of Yarmouth ahead, yacht masts and church tower. At the end of the sea wall we turn onto the road and over the bridge into the town – or, if it is summertime, take the ferry.

For the ferry, walk from the sea wall straight ahead onto the sandy point called Norton Spit, with the sea on one side and a marshy lagoon on the other, a favourite place for waders such as redshank, dunlin and curlew. The small, open ferry boat will pick you up and take you across the harbour with a close view of the yachts, fishing boats, visiting trawlers, car ferry and lifeboat, to the quayside.

Much of the westward traffic has been routed round Yarmouth, so in spite of the ferry terminal it is an interesting and pleasant old town to walk round.

Right beside the ferry entrance and tucked away up an alleyway stands one of the lesser-known glories of the island, Yarmouth Castle. It was built by Henry VIII on the site of a church destroyed in a French raid, to repel any more such invasions. This is not a ruin but a small, almost cosy, complete castle where you can wander up and down stairs, sit on the wide windowseats in parlour and kitchen and eventually reach the large gun platform, a perfect picnic place with a splendid view of the harbour and the Solent.

Past the castle we reach the square. On the left the newly restored wooden pier offers another sea view, for walkers only. The town hall dated 1763 stands on the west side, with Jireh House nearby, a century older. The George Hotel which occupies the old castle grounds was once the home of Sir Robert Holmes, Governor of the island. Here he entertained Charles II – there is a plaque to mark the King's bedroom. From its garden you can see the splendidly carved coat of arms of Henry VIII over the original east door.

At the south side of the square stands the church, its plain square tower a landmark for miles around, rebuilt in the seventeenth century. Do not miss the statue of Sir Robert Holmes within. He captured a French ship in the Channel, part of its cargo being an unfinished statue of Louis XIV of France. This he brought back to Yarmouth, where he had his own head sculptured onto it so that it could be erected at his death in 1692.

Small shops line the narrow streets, many with an eye to the yacht trade. In summer there are boat trips from the harbour for fishing expeditions or to view the Needles at close quarters.

To find the Coastal Path again, cross the square and turn east along the narrow High Street till it reaches a grassy bank, a long grandstand to the Solent, with plenty of seats. A path leads down the grass to the sea wall, which continues to the edge of the town, where we must take to the road for a few hundred yards, passing the Mediterranean roofs of Port La Salle and ignoring a footpath down its drive which leads to the beach but not to the Coastal Path.

The Coastal Path turns off to the left a little further on, down a gravel road passing a few houses to a signpost pointing seaward, the beginning of a delightful, little-used stretch. The path crosses a footbridge into a wood of gnarled oaks and hazels, lovely in spring when the primroses are out, and presently leads down to beach-level, skirting a small bay defined by a broken jetty at its further point, backed by a reed-bed excellent for bird-watching – cormorants use the jetty for wing-drying. Beyond the bay, the path climbs again and turns inland slightly through a pine wood – look for tin arrows on tree trunks. The path used to follow the cliff edge but this constantly falls. [By the time you read this, directions may have changed again, but they will certainly be signposted.] At any time of year the way can be very muddy after wet weather, and boots are probably advisable.

Where the path returns to the cliff edge, it climbs past a look-out left over from the last war, once a starkly functional brick box, now picturesquely bowered in ivy. Another pine wood brings us to a seat at the cliff edge, looking down over a vast cliff fall, bare slurries of wet clay gradually being reclaimed by birch and gorse. All along we are never far from the sea, while inland, woods stretch south, quiet and green. [Various paths lead off inland, eventually coming out on the Yarmouth to Shalfleet road.]

Look back along the coast, right across Yarmouth to Fort Victoria on the point opposite Hurst Castle; the channel between looks very narrow from here. Across the water, Sway Tower pierces the skyline from the edge of the New Forest. A red warning notice draws attention to a permanent diversion where the old path has disappeared over the cliff, and a signpost points toward Shalfleet, down through the pines and over a stile, across the grass in front of a bungalow, over another stile onto a gravel road, West Close. This is the hamlet of Cranmore, where a vineyard is hidden away. Soon, reaching Cranmore Avenue, we turn left and almost at once right, down Solent Road, soon losing the scattered houses.

Here we have joined the Hamstead Trail described in detail on pp.144-9. The path leads on past Pigeon Coo Farm to a narrow road. Turn left along it and soon right through woods and fields down to the shore at Newtown Creek – a pleasant spot but, for those devoted to the Coastal Path, a dead end. You have to retrace your steps to Pigeon Coo.

For those who do not want to take this extra walk, turn right along the narrow road, downhill to a stone bridge over an arm of the creek. Almost at once a footpath leads off left through the woods, to an enchanting little stretch of the creek, mudflats and quiet waters all overhung with oak woods, little natural lawns along the bank ideal for picnics or bird-watching, a water vole swimming past or maybe a pair of swans. The path bends to the right through a fringe of trees, to a wooden footbridge – be warned: this stretch is often very muddy. Once across, we keep the hedge on our left and skirt the bottom of the field, following the hedge on round in a long, gentle climb which eventually brings us out onto the Yarmouth to Shalfleet road, where we turn left for half a mile, then downhill into the village. The church to the south, with squat, fort-like tower, was built by the Normans, though it has also a very up-to-date stained glass window, a war memorial, depicting an aeroplane and a submarine.

Opposite stands the New Inn, where pub snacks include fresh sea-food. We turn down beside it. Straight ahead through a gate lies the track to Shalfleet Quay with its seventeenth-century stone walls and clutter of small boats, but the Coastal Path swings round across a bridge over the Caul Bourne, between the old mill and the old bakery which together supplied much of west Wight with flour and bread until the 1920s. The stream is widening out to a creek, with a glimpse of boats beyond. Uphill through a small wood, the path soon reaches a tarmac lane which leads out to the Shalfleet to Newtown road. The next two miles are eastward along roads, but they are quiet and wooded for the most part, with little traffic.

To explore ancient Newtown, turn left at the bridge, otherwise keep straight on to a tiny green triangle where four lanes meet – London Heath! We carry straight on downhill through an avenue of huge old oak trees to a bridge over yet one more arm of the creek, called Clamerkins. Lean over the bridge for a glimpse of yellow-breasted grey wagtail or kingfisher. Close by is Clamerkins Farm Park, open to visitors in summer. Uphill we keep left round the bend, leaving the woods now for the hamlet of Locks Heath. Facing the green stands a beautiful double-gabled old house often taken to be a manor – in fact, it is the old schoolhouse elegantly done up.

Another half mile of road brings us to Porchfield. Opposite the pub, the Sportsman's Rest, a lane with a cul-de-sac sign leads in a mile and a half to the Solent shore. But this is only a detour, and we should have to return to Porchfield. So, leaving the pub and general store on the right, we begin to climb gently up Bunts Hill, and there at last is the blue Coastal Footpath sign, pointing off the road, saying '3 miles to Gurnard'. With the hedge on our right and heading for the sea, we walk through three fields, now climbing towards Great Thorness Farm, but before reaching it, bear right, through the fence to a rough road. Turn left up it for a few yards, then right towards Thorness Bay, over a stile and into Pilgrims Park Holiday Camp where the road brings us to a long fieldpath to the shore.

All this north shore from Yarmouth to Gurnard is some way from a road, so unspoiled and wild: small crumbling cliffs, mud and sand, bleached tree trunks fallen from above, reefs of rock stretching far out at low tide, splendid prawning grounds. A quarter of a mile brings us to a stream, then the way climbs the cliff and over a stile. The path follows the cliff edge to Gurnard now, over various stiles, through gorse thickets, bramble and teazle, slippery after rain, with a view right across the Solent to the mouth of Beaulieu River. Downhill, roofs come into sight. We climb a last stile and turn right a few yards to come out onto Gurnard Marsh, beside a stream mouth full of small boats.

Crossing the bridge we take the road through the marsh, which is covered with holiday chalets, and climb Solent View Road straight ahead, turning left at the T-junction. Worsley Road appears to come to an abrupt end high above the sea, but when you get there the road is seen to narrow to half its width and turn sharp right down a precipitous hill. Round the bend it does head steeply straight down to the shore, but one more turn right brings us to Gurnard Bay and the beginning of a fine all-season walk into Cowes, flat, paved and easy though right by the sea, ideal for prams and wheelchairs, a gentle stroll to end the Coastal footpath.

Cars can park facing the Solent above a grassy slope, wooded on the west, dropping down to a line of small beach huts, with a view west into Gurnard Bay – a small, homely seaside place much used by the local people. There are seats ideal for picnics on the green, a scatter of boats and sailboards on the grass, several cafés, a narrow beach.

Princes Parade begins at the foot of the green, the result of a job-creation scheme in the slump years of the 1920s; before that only a muddy path along the shoreline joined Gurnard to Cowes. Opened by the Prince of Wales in 1926, it is a

marvellous viewpoint for big events such as the start of the
Fastnet Yacht Race, the Powerboat Race and the events of
Cowes Week, but there are always some craft to be seen at
any time of year.

The beach below becomes a mere jumble of wrack-covered
rocks, lacing the breeze with a strong tang of the sea. Now
and then the wide pavement broadens out into half-moon
bays with seats facing the Solent and the mainland beyond,
Calshott Spit and the mouth of Southampton Water. Behind,
across the road, the rough clay slope is covered with oak and
thorn scrub, boughs all combed inland by the wind off the
sea. Though the promenade is flat, it is by no means straight:
one walks on a gentle curve all the time so that every step
widens the view.

Soon the stretch of water called Cowes Roads comes in
sight, with great tankers moored, waiting to sail up to Fawley
oil refinery, whose chimneys can be seen rearing up from
Southampton Water; there are also cargo boats and, of
course, many yachts. A small automatic lighthouse resembling an upturned dumb-bell with a pink stem marks Egypt
Point. From here the promenade carries on beside the sea into
the heart of Cowes, which is explored on pp.37-8.

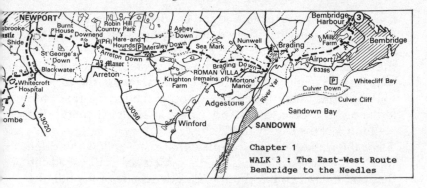

Chapter 1
WALK 3 : The East-West Route
Bembridge to the Needles

Walk 3: The East-West Route: Bembridge to the Needles
Distance: 35 miles (56 kilometres)
Map: *see* pp.38-9

Our second long-distance walk, the east-west route, crosses the whole island from Bembridge harbour to the Needles along the spines of the downs, with a detour round Newport.

At Bembridge we start off by the harbour at the Pilot Boat Inn, an unmistakable landmark built to look like a ship with portholes. Take the track leading past it into the woods, with glimpses of 'lakes' through the trees, actually flooded gravelpits but beloved of pochard, mallard, shoveller and tufted duck. Take a turning uphill to the left, coming out onto a road where we turn right and make for Bembridge Windmill. Smugglers once used the set of its huge sails to send code messages to each other, such as 'Not safe to land tubs tonight'.

From here the path to Brading High Street is described on pp.63-6. It crosses the marshes reclaimed from the sea to Wall Lane and Brading High Street, where we turn left through the village to the Bull Ring at the top, cross over and walk up The Mall. Here we can take the track to the right leading into Nunwell Woods (pp.66-7) and scramble up one of the steep chalk paths onto the down summit, or walk right along the road to a narrow turning right to visit Morton Manor or Brading Roman villa. The straightforward route to find the beginning of the Downland Way is to continue up The Mall to the United Reform Church and take the steep road opposite which climbs quickly up onto the downs. Ignore the turn off to Adgestone and a pit entrance and make for the first path left, onto the open grassland where a signpost marks the beginning of the Downland Way.

For the walker, it is unfortunate that roads follow the ridge tops of the eastern downs. The long-distance path called the Bembridge Trail swaps about from side to side of the hill; the newer Downland Way closely follows the road: one is never far from traffic but the views are superb. It leads along grassy downland rich in chalk-loving flowers such as cowslip and mullein and hundreds of wayfaring trees which blossom in May, with a view down onto Adgestone Vineyard below and behind to the great headland of Culver with the Solent beyond.

Over a stile the land is more overgrown with gorse and thorn, a place for yellowhammers. Picnic places are scattered about. A gate leads to a small car-park where we cross the road and then, for a long stretch, walk along a wide grass verge with a view opening out ahead right across to west Wight downs, with the roofs and churches of Ryde far below on the north, and straight ahead a large white pillar, like a truncated pyramid; this is Ashey Sea Mark, twenty feet high, put up in 1735 as a marker for shipping entering St Helen's Roads.

On a sharp bend, we have to cross the road. Now the path has a hedge between it and the road. Various side paths shoot off southward to Knighton or Arreton in the valley below. Past one of these our path takes to the verge again, with views along the down's steep flank and onto the tops of woods below, while larks sing above. Where the road makes a T-junction, turn left, keeping to the verge. Here the path sinks below road-level with a high bank on the right and a vast view over the flat Vale of Arreton below. When the sun glints on the greenhouses or fields covered with polythene, the vale appears strewn with silver lakes. Soon we are looking down onto the old nucleus of Arreton, church, farm and manor. Skirting a vast chalk pit, the Downland Way ends near a pub well known for its food, the Hare and Hounds. Its other claim to fame is a beam that once formed part of the gibbet of Micah Morey, who murdered his grandson James, with a hatchet, was tried and duly hanged up here on the hill.

At the junction, go down the hill on the left, then turn along a lane opposite the entrance to the chalkpit. (Alternatively you could walk on down to the bottom of the hill and take a path on the right signposted St George's Down, or take time off to visit Arreton Manor, a beautiful stone house built in 1639 but incorporating some of the original farmhouse built by the monks of Quarr Abbey.) Burnt House Lane, our way ahead, is narrow and pretty, tarmac but with little traffic, winding up and down through a fold in the hills, between high banks, and a few farms; at one point we can look down onto the roofs of Newport.

Reaching a wider lane, we turn left and quickly right. (The track over St George's Down also joins in here.) This has brought us to Shide and a busy roundabout. Cross over, with care, to the gate giving onto the streamside path described on pp.102-3 and signposted Blackwater. Follow the stream to Blackwater and turn right to Whitecroft Hospital, then left along the road for a short distance till a lane leads uphill on the right. Climb up past Hill Farm, then steeply downhill to Gatcombe, turning right along its narrow 'high street' and keeping straight on at the junction of paths below the kennels.

Now we are in a dim lane, deep sunken between high banks draped with ferns and moss, overhung with trees, a green tunnel – Snowdrop Lane, once white with the little flowers in early spring though now only a few clumps remain. Climbing into more open country, we take a left-hand fork through the farm. (A delightful track goes off on the left leading to the summit of Garstons Down and to

Shorwell.) A long, straight path with a hedge on the right leads up to the road from Carisbrooke to Shorwell, in the hamlet of Bowcombe. Just to the right, a lane leads off opposite, climbing between deep hedges to skirt a wood, quite steep. Past the shady slopes it veers round to the right and comes up across fields to join the main bridleway on Bowcombe Down, where we turn left to join this lovely ridgewalk all the way to the Needles.

For those who wish to pick up the Tennyson Trail at its beginning, in Carisbrooke, pass the church and carry straight on across the crossroads for some 200 yards, but just before the climb grows really steep, fork left up a tarmac lane called Nodgham. Another few yards brings us to the beginning of the footpath proper on the right, a track climbing between high banks sometimes overhung with trees till it levels out on a wide stretch of grass, Little Down, good for chalk-loving scabious and knapweed. This narrows to a path again leading to a gate onto Bowcombe Down, and a crossroads of lanes. White Lane goes down to the Shorwell Road. The path to the right leads over the summit and past a pit known as the Frying Pan. This area was once covered with wild raspberry bushes, some with yellow fruit, but they were lost when the downland turf was put under plough during the last war – it has been kept under cultivation ever since. On the north side the path leads out onto the Calbourne road, right opposite the Blacksmith's Arms, which does nice food.

To keep on the Tennyson Trail, we carry straight on along the ridge with a wide view of central Wight spread out below, then, as the down narrows, enter a lane. Just beyond this the path from Bowcombe on our walk from Bembridge joins in. We are gradually nearing the tree-filled Rowridge valley, till we are right beside old woods of beech and oak, carpeted with bluebells or fringed with foxgloves in their season.

The next section used to lie between wide thickets, their banks a riot of wild flowers until the farmer tore out the sheltering thorn bushes and put the land under plough, making this section of path rather a bleak slog. But now the north side has been replanted, this time with beech, chestnut and larch, which in years to come will bring back the vetches and campions. This stretch can be muddy at any time of year and, if the Forestry Commission have been working in the plantations ahead, really needs boots, though once west of Brighstone the going is firm and good on undisturbed chalk.

Across the valley stands the tall TV mast of BBC Rowridge; the track then keeps along a fence with vast fields rolling away on either side, full of gambolling lambs in spring. Through a gateway we join the first Forestry Commission plantation, skirting along its edge. The old gloomy pine trees have been felled and little new ones planted, but the next gateway leads into a long stretch of path with young beech woods on either side, even meeting overhead, a complete change of scene which lasts till a gate comes in right onto a rough chalk road and we burst out of the trees onto Brighstone Down with all the south-west coast laid out below, with the sea beyond, St Catherine's Down on the east and the far white cliffs of Freshwater beckoning us westward.

(To visit Brighstone village, turn left and walk along to a signposted gate on the right, then down a green road to pick up the path coming from Row Down.)

For the Tennyson Trail, we turn right along the chalk road and descend to a road crossing from Brighstone to Calbourne. Walking straight across, we regain the downs, here called Westover, where sheep are often pastured as part of the management plan of the National Trust, so dogs must go on leads. Westover is a long, slow climb with lovely open views to the south, forestry to the north, till we reach the summit and the remains of five Bronze Age barrows, long ago pillaged of their contents but worth climbing for the new view of north-west Wight and the Solent.

Then the track descends slowly through cowslip slopes to cross the Brook road. Opposite a lane leads on toward Brook Down, crossing the Hamstead Trail going north. Through the gate, a white track terraces up the side of the hill to the top. Once there, it is a splendid level ridge walk, with widening

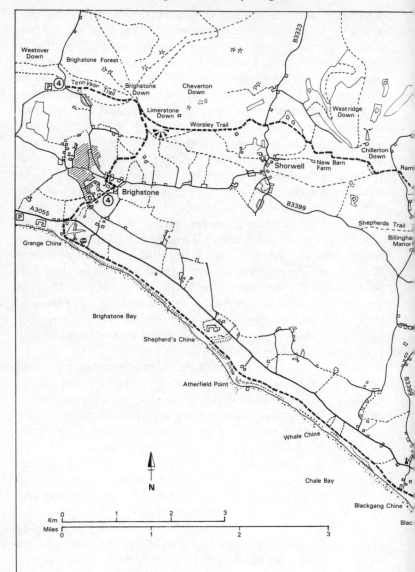

Chapter 1

WALK 4 : Brighstone to Ventnor circular

views of the coasts both north and south as the island narrows. Many chalk-loving plants grow up here, but they tend to be dwarfed by the sea winds. Several gates lead eventually to Freshwater golf course (please keep to the right of way) and a view down into the bay. Keep left and walk down into a car-park, and cross the Military Road to join the Coastal Path. This breaks off abruptly at the cliff edge, just above the great gull-haunted stacks, Arch, Stag and Mermaid Rocks, where steps lead down into white-walled Freshwater Bay. From here we join the Coastal Path described on pp.28-30 to reach the island's western most cliffs and the Needles.

Walk 4: Brighstone to Ventnor circular
Distance: 21 miles (33.6 kilometres)
Map: *see* pp.44-5

The Worsley Trail stretches from Brighstone across the down to Shanklin, occasionally plunging down into river valleys for a complete change of scenery. Leave your car in the National Trust car-park on Westover Down and cross the road to a lane leading out onto a chalk track heading east over the down or, if walking from Brighstone village, take Sandy Lane described on p.129-31 to the summit of the down, joining the white track further east.

We continue eastward along it, with a vast coastal view over to St Catherine's Down, larks singing and turf studded with little chalk-loving flowers such as eyebright and dwarf thistles. The track gradually swings round to the north, leaving Brighstone Forest boundary, and a small radar station comes into view. This is a testing point for Plessey, who have a large works at Northwood, a modern intrusion upon an ancient track. Everywhere else on the downs are the grassy hollows of old chalkpits, often ideal for picnics, but ahead is the stark white scar of a new pit still in constant use.

Keep along the main track, and beside a pond go right, through a gate, into a metalled lane between high banks, which comes out at the tops of the 'shute' or steep main road plunging down to Shorwell. A great bowl of land on the right turns white with garlic flowers in May – it can be smelt all around. Cross the road and take a bridleway signposted to Chillerton. This is a firm, wide track leading up to a wood and all along its southern edge, a place bright with bluebells, stitchwort and campion in spring, where pheasants often rocket up from your feet. Just inside the wood grows the yellow form of archangel, known on the island by the endearing name of weaselsnout.

The path follows round the end of the wood and along a short length of fence to a gate into a big sloping meadow with the buildings of New Barn Farm at its foot. Walk about half way down, then turn left towards a signpost by the bank. Beyond the farm, rising land folds in the valley, a lovely green, hidden place. We climb the steep bank thick with cowslips in May, go through a small gate and follow a fence along to a fieldgate leading to the foot of the down under the tall TV mast. The going here can be very rough, trampled by cattle and dried to potholes. We keep along by a series of old chalkpits, looking out toward the Channel coast and St Catherine's, then turn onto a track between high hedges which comes out on the main road between Carisbrooke and Chale. Here we turn right for a short distance to the next turning left.

A narrow tarmac lane along the downside looking down on the hamlet of Billingham, whose manor house is said to be haunted by the ghost of King Charles I – only his head appears. Many farmers in this area grow oil-seed rape as a crop, so that in spring some of the chequered squares below are as brilliant a yellow as any bulb fields. The sheltered bank facing south often yields the first primroses of the year. Where the lane swings round a sharp bend, a view of north Wight comes in sight briefly before the lane bends again, downhill past Ramsdown Farm, where the Shepherd's Trail, coming up from the coast and heading for Carisbrooke, crosses this one. Deep banks close us in, ending at a

T-junction where we turn right a short way to Roslin Farm, where the path turns in left past the farm buildings, through a gate onto a track. We continue on the same way to Cridmore Farm. Passing this and ignoring turnings off, we come to the end of the track in a field and cross to another gate on the opposite side of the field and then, with hedge on right, bear left to a track which leads to 'The Wilderness'.

This is a delightful strip of marshy copse along the banks of the infant River Medina, overhung with old oaks. Duck and moorhen nest in the reedbeds. Foxgloves flourish, with yellow iris, marsh marigolds and rarer plants, bright dragonflies darting among them in summer. A small gate leads to a one-plank bridge over the stream, narrow here but immediately widening out below. Follow the hedge round two angles to a lane; ignore this and continue up the valley with the hedge on the left, through a gate, then turn left and left again to climb a field verge and arrive on the road crossing Bleak Down.

Turn right along the road for nearly half a mile, a high ridge walk looking out over St Catherine's Down and the Channel. At a pair of gates on the left, take the further one signposted to Godshill and a track veering right to another gate. Turn right downhill, looking for a cottage in the dip. Keeping this on our right, we reach a corner where a small gate immediately gives onto another leading left to a signpost to Godshill.

The path passes through one more wicket gate, then slopes gently downhill, with pasture fields on one side, a hedge on the other, and a view straight ahead to Godshill church on its mound, finally turning right into the narrow sunken lane known as Beacon Alley, its deep banks green with moss, fern and pennywort's green leather buttons. We turn left along it, cross a bridge over the infant River Yar and come to the wide road from Godshill to Whitwell. Here we cross over and almost at once turn left up a tarmac lane to a T-junction. The left-hand turn would take us down to Godshill village, but we are for the heights and turn right a short way to Sainham

Farm, where we turn left through a field and gate, straight ahead along a track with the farm to the left. The route keeps straight ahead now, with meadows to one side. On the other the down is cut off above us by the dramatic sudden fall of Gat Cliff.

Here we leave the Worsley Trail. (It continues on to Wroxall, climbs the downs by the route described the other way round in Chapter VII, retraces part of that ridge walk, then turns off eastwards to end at St Blasius' Church in Shanklin Olde Village.) Our route continues as the Stenbury Trail, south-eastwards, turning right along the north side of the Appuldurcombe estate wall, keeping beside it, climbing Stenbury Down to a gate. Through this we bear right along the track, passing some GPO pylons. This is a splendid open ridge walk over Stenbury and Week Downs. Paths lead down westward to the hamlet of Nettlecombe and to Whitwell, eastward to Wroxall, but we keep southward along the ridge through several gates. From here the whole of southern Wight is laid out below like a map, a real coastal panorama. Though St Boniface Down is higher, its own bulk blocks off such extensive views as this.

At the signpost we begin to descend a narrow path through thickets of bramble and blackthorn, slowly coming round the flank of a vast natural amphitheatre, Watcombe Bottom.

When Apollo pursued Daphne with amorous intent, she took root and turned into a plant to spite him: daphne grows here, flowering as early as January; and wild madder sprawls between gorse stems like an outsize goosegrass.

The green summit of the inner cliff comes into view, then far below the tree-tops of the Undercliff and the sea. The path goes through the sports centre out onto the road from Ventnor to Whitwell. We can turn left for Ventnor, about a mile along the road, or cross over onto the Coastal Path and walk along it through Niton, Blackgang and Chale to Grange Chine, where a footpath through the fields turns off just beyond the road turn leading in about a mile to Brighstone village.

II   East and North-East Wight

This is the most tamed part of the island, with Ryde its most sophisticated town and many prosperous houses built round about from Georgian times onward, but there is still a wide variety of walking country from hanging woods to sea meadows, from flowery marshes to the great chalk headland of Culver plunging to the sea.

Ryde is a busy shopping town and, as ferry port for London, has good communications with the rest of the island, a bus station at the foot of the pier and trains to Shanklin, which make it a good walking centre for those without cars. Southern Vectis issue Ramblers' Tickets in summer, one payment giving you freedom of the bus network for a week. East Wight will suit walkers with small children, or older people who want to see the country but can never be too far from a café or bus stop, while the more adventurous can combine several walks into day-long expeditions.

Walk 1: Firestone Copse
Distance: 1¾ miles (2.8 kilometres)
Map: *see* p.52

To explore the hinterland of Ryde, catch a bus to Wootton, five miles away, one of the oldest villages on the island, sprawling among woods either side of the wide creek. The long bridge across was originally the causeway of a dam built for the tide-mill which stood beside the Sloop Inn. The view seaward is of boatyards, yachts at anchor, dinghies plying to and fro, but to the south the creek widens out into a shining lake between quiet green fields and woods, one of them Firestone Copse.

To reach it, keep on the bus-stop side of the road, walk back across the bridge and a few yards up Kite Hill turn right into Firestone Road, in fact a narrow, winding lane which soon enters the woods. Three-quarters of a mile lead to the Firestone entrance, which the Forestry Commission have recently much improved. Car-parking is divided among little clearings, a grassy stretch has benches for picnics, and there is a map of the copse showing the routes of three different walks, the red route a mere quarter-mile potter, yellow one mile and green 1¾ miles. Of course, you can walk where you like and spend all day exploring the various gravel tracks and narrower paths. In spring there are glades full of little wild daffodils; in summer the air is fragrant with meadowsweet in the wet ditches and verges bright with vetches, orchids and the small lilac-flowered thistles which smell of honey.

The green route curves away through the trees, a wide, gravelled track with little side paths shooting off among the oak and birch. Soon a red arrow on the left points the way to circle back for the shortest route, fine for wheelchairs and prams. We walk on into a wood of Scots pine, sloping away

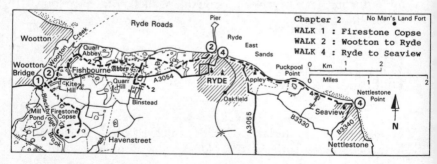

toward the headwaters of Wootton Creek, as yet invisible. Rounding a bend, the track stretches away ahead with a yellow arrow. We follow the green left onto a much narrower path downhill through a grove of young cypress to level out beside the creek, and wander on just inside the cover of twisted oaks for a long stretch, crossing a rustic bridge, with benches placed in gaps so you can sit and bird-watch in comfort right out over the flat marshes and reedbeds with narrow channels winding through them, home to duck, waders and gulls.

Underfoot, wood ants are busy, and scatters of cone scales show that squirrels have been active: in fact, it is worth turning your back on the creek and sitting quietly, looking into the depths of the wood, for all the squirrels on the Isle of Wight are the beautiful red ones – none of those grey interlopers! The last seat is on a small bluff; if the sluices are closed at Wootton Bridge, it overlooks a shining lake, but if they are open, banks of grey mud. As a consolation, the mud is more likely to attract birds in to feed.

Now the green arrow points away from the creek, so we turn right uphill and then left onto a wide grassy track and right again, a narrow way through pines back to beeches and oaks with a few larch. A few more twists and turns following the green arrow bring us back to the car-park or Firestone Lane leading back to Wootton.

Walk 2: Wootton to Ryde
Distance: 3½ miles (5.6 kilometres)
Map: *see* p.52

The second walk from Wootton leads to Ryde. This is also a convenient place to start on the coastal path leading right round the island, since the previous stretch is forced onto tarmac roads away from the sea by large private estates and is hardly worth walking, whereas Wootton right round to Cowes is a splendid long-distance tramp with very little road work.

Kite Hill is always very busy. We cross, from the pavement on the south side, with care, and dive thankfully down a path signposted to Fishbourne. Such a different world so quickly, green and tree hung – even the house has the enchanting country name of Squirrels' Leap.

Soon the gravel gives way to a narrow and often muddy copse path which comes out onto a tarmac lane which we follow till a notice says 'No More Public Access', and a narrow grassy way on the right leads up into Fishbourne Lane, where we turn left, passing the vast car-park and jetty of the Sea Link Car Ferry from Portsmouth. Soon there is a footpath signposted to Binstead. (Nearly all island signposts are green with white letters; only the coastal footpath signs are blue.) It is worth a short detour to the beach, so carry straight on.

The road ends in a charming little round green with a large oak tree in the centre surrounded by a circular seat. Across it a track leads down to a pebble beach with another small green and seats overlooking the wooded creek mouth and boat jetties. The car ferry looms enormous among the small yachts sailing to and fro and sends a powerful wash storming up the beach.

We retrace our steps to the signpost opposite the Fishbourne Inn and turn along a lane into the country of the monks.

The abbey of Our Lady of Quarr was founded in 1132. This path leads to its ruins, through a gate, between high hedges and sweet chestnuts, cascades of flower in July when most trees are over. Soon, above the trees appear rose-red towers and turrets in strange Eastern shapes – this is the new Quarr Abbey, built of warm Flemish brick in 1907. Keeping straight on, skirting the abbey orchard and disregarding any turnings, you may meet a black-robed monk clipping the hedge or driving a tractor.

Go straight across the drive unless you wish to visit the impressive church, the only part of the abbey open to the public, in which case turn left. Walking on past the signpost to Binstead, our route becomes more open and sunny and passes under a stone archway, entrance to the original monastery. Only ten monks remained by Henry VIII's time, and, at his dissolution of the monasteries they begged to be left in peace: 'Fifty souls do we maintain regularly – let alone outsiders from all the country round.' But the house was dissolved by the King's order just the same, and much of the stone was carted away to build forts along the Solent. We can see what is left as we walk on, some walls incorporated into a fine farmhouse, while in the sea meadows beyond, black-and-white cattle graze among the fragments of wall, the stone outline of a window, a gateway.

Past the ruins, our way becomes more tree-hung, and houses appear among ancient oak trees on the outskirts of Binstead, once famous for its quarries, hence the name Quarr (rhyming with or). Where we meet tarmac at a T-junction there is a narrow and easily missed little path forking off left which makes a pleasant detour to the beach (for all this is the coastal footpath, we have not seen much sea). A quarter-mile through the woods brings us out onto the shore. True it is pebbles, with low tide revealing mud and rocks, but there is a lovely view of the Solent, with big ships manoeuvring to sail up Southampton Water, ferries coming into Ryde Pier, while near at hand oyster-catchers and curlew case the tide-line.

Back on our walk, we follow old walls round to the left, passing Binstead church with a curious stone figure, said to be a heathen idol, over its stone gateway and down a short, steep hill to a bridge over a stream. You can follow it to find the beach again, but we take the path uphill. All the ground between church and main road was once quarries, providing stone for Winchester Cathedral and Beaulieu Abbey, but long overgrown now and built over. Soon we are passing slap through the middle of Ryde golf course, but well protected by high hedges. This is called Ladies' Walk and brings us out close to the main road. Cross a drive and go through a white wicket gate signposted to Ryde onto a narrow path which soon broadens out into a quiet road.

Walk 3: Ryde Town Trail
Time: Allow 1½ hours
Map: *see* p.57

Though we are back in Ryde, the way is still full of interest, for this was where prosperous Victorians built their florid mansions, vying with the nearby royal residence at Osborne in towers, turrets and castellations.

Ryde was originally two villages, the higher one joined to the cluster of fisherman's huts near the sea, by a narrow lane, and grew into a town only after the land was acquired by the Player family early in the nineteenth century. After that it grew quickly and flowered as a fashionable resort: it is one of fifty towns in Britain selected for the excellence of its Victorian buildings, and before walking on to Seaview, a town trail makes an interesting contrast to the previous walks.

Spencer Road leads to St Thomas' Street, where we turn left downhill to the esplanade, from which we climb up Union Street, which eventually united the two villages. Above the shops are Regency and Georgian fronts, the very tallest on the right surmounted by a row of statues. Just beyond it, we turn into the Royal Victoria Arcade, recently restored from dereliction and now lined with boutiques selling antiques, jewellery and Victorian bric-à-brac. At weekends there is a stall market in the cellars beneath. At the far end, we go through doors into narrow Church Lane and uphill, past a high stone wall, to St Thomas's Church, built by Thomas Player in 1827. The churchyard has been laid out as a small park with bright flowerbeds and seats on a brick patio, a pleasant oasis in the heart of the town. For years the stone church with its handsome tower was derelict, with broken windows and ivy-shrouded walls, but now it has taken on a new role. Restored to its former glory, it houses an exhibition mounted by the British Australian Heritage Society, opened by the Queen in 1987. This commemorates the sailing of the first fleet to Australia, which set sail from the Mother Bank, off Ryde in 1787.

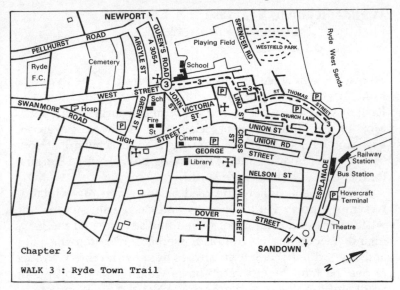

Chapter 2

WALK 3 : Ryde Town Trail

From St Thomas's turn right along Lind Street, past the elegant town hall with its clocktower built in 1827. At the end of the road, All Saints' can be seen at the top of the hill. It is still a flourishing church, designed by Sir Gilbert Scott in 1867, its tall spire dominating the town and a landmark from the sea. On return we descend the road on the west side of St Thomas's to see Brigstocke Terrace, flats now but originally a row of Regency houses, erected by another family which held sway in the town. The Brigstockes also left a superb collection of oriental china to Ryde, which is sometimes on display.

The road curves downhill, past the pillared front of the Royal Victoria Yacht Club, its foundation stone laid by Prince Albert in 1846, back to the sea front and the pier. Built in 1824, it made a regular ferry service possible for the first time: previously passengers had to be brought in on horsedrawn carts when the tide was low. Though much altered, the pier retains some Victorian wrought iron and still makes a pleasant promenade for watching the ever-changing shipping in the Solent.

Walk 4: Ryde to Seaview
Distance: 2½ miles (4 kilometres)
Map: *see* p.52

To reach Seaview we set out along the length of the Ryde sea front, past many large hotels, a train and bus station, the Eastern Gardens with their theatre and a large canoe lake. Most of this land has been reclaimed from the sea; even so, vast sandbanks stretch out nearly a mile seaward at low spring tides, inviting and safe-looking but very treacherous, for the sea surges back with speed.

At the far end, where the road narrows and turns inland, we enter Appley Park. This is a flat, easy walk suitable for wheelchairs and prams, yet with a fine sea view all the way. Inland, woods stretch uphill, flowerbeds brighten the path and beyond lies the Solent, always busy with cross-Channel ferries, oil tankers and cargo boats waiting for moorings in Southampton Water, and grey Royal Naval craft in and out of Portsmouth Harbour opposite. The path is on a high sea wall which soon brings into sight the forts built out in the Solent against a potential French invasion in the 1860s – great round islands now known as Palmerston's Follies. No Man's Fort is the nearest, with Horse Sand beyond, nearer the mainland shore; St Helen's Fort is further east.

Just before we come out onto a road at Puckpool, a turn to the right leads to the overgrown remains of another large Victorian gun battery, now part of Puckpool Park. Beside it the path joins the toll road where motorists must pay 10 pence for the pleasure of driving along right by the sea. Wild bird cries from inland mean we are near Flamingo Park, ten acres of coastal hillside sloping down to marshland, inspired by a visit to Sir Peter Scott's Slimbridge, where many kinds of duck rub shoulders with more exotic fowl and the flamingo themselves. This area was once utilized as salterns – flat, shallow pools where salt water could be evaporated by the sun.

Where the road swerves inland, our route once more

becomes a sea wall, but it is worth walking a few yards up the road to see the picturesque old saltern cottages, for there is not much else of antiquity in Seaview. The route continues along into the village, then veers inland to a road skirting the landward side of Seaview Yacht Club, then back to the sea front proper past the Old Fort Inn, all cluttered with small boats and boat trolleys in summer.

After Ryde, Seaview has a rural charm, little steep streets and alleyways leading to the sea. Most of the village dates only from about 1800, when the Caws family bought a large field and divided it into cottage plots for themselves. If you want to be fitted for walking shoes in the old-fashioned leisurely way, visit Caws shoe shop, still run by the family.

Walk 5: Seaview to St Helens
Distance: 1½ miles (2.4 kilometres)
Map: *see* p.60

From the foot of the High Street, the sea wall seems to continue on towards Priory Bay, but the last few yards of ground are private, so you have to go down steps onto the beach. This is all right at low tide but at high tide is impossible. Our way then lies up the High Street and along the second road to the left, but turn round first for a view of the Solent framed in High Street with No Man's Land Fort dead centre and the white mini-skyscrapers of the mainland opposite, a nice contrast to Seaview village. The road soon becomes a wide but pot-holed track down into Priory Bay – cars can be parked here.

The sea has pounded a concrete sea wall into car-size chunks and thrown them up against each other at drunken angles. Here stood the entrance to the pier, which resembled a suspension bridge in design and enabled a direct link by boat with Portsmouth during its heyday as a resort for the gentry. Closed and neglected during the last war, the pier was finally destroyed by a great storm in 1951. More ruins on

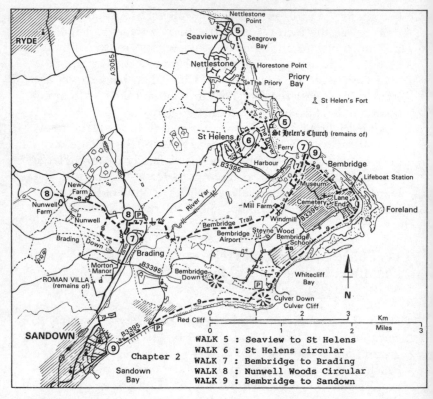

WALK 5 : Seaview to St Helens
WALK 6 : St Helens circular
WALK 7 : Bembridge to Brading
WALK 8 : Nunwell Woods Circular
WALK 9 : Bembridge to Sandown

Chapter 2

the land side are the remains of a modern hotel pulled down but never rebuilt and used in summer as an unofficial dinghy park.

The broken wall provides a lovely view of Priory Bay, a small sandy crescent half within the wooded and encircling arm of Horestone Point, with the further point of Foreland beyond, unmistakable from its long jetty leading to Bembridge lifeboat station. Past an old cottage we turn up a short green lane into a road running along the backs of seaside houses, with glimpses of the sea, which soon narrows to a footpath leading to a T-junction.

Downhill leads back to the beach. If the tide is ebbing, it is possible to walk round to St Helens on the beach, threading between rocks on firm sand, but do take local advice about when to set out: the tide does go out a long way here but, when it turns, comes in with sinister speed. Uphill along Fernclose and past the cul-de-sac sign is the real coastal route – a steep climb, and the tarmac peters out, becoming a rutted track with houses secluded in their own grounds. Where a lane joins from the right, we turn left down a footpath overhung with trees, actually skirting the grounds of what is now the Priory Hotel.

The Normans founded a priory right by the shore at St Helens, suppressed in 1414 since it belonged to the alien French, though the church remained. When the monks' home disappeared, their farmhouse took on the name of Priory. In the following centuries it was much enlarged, almost rebuilt, and today is an hotel. Legend tells of the original priory's treasure, hidden in its cellars!

We come out onto the main drive and turn downhill, then through a stone gateway onto a road. A further short distance downhill and an iron gate, signposted to Bembridge, gives onto a sloping meadow where horses often graze – ignore them and they ignore you. There are shining glimpses of the harbour, and the headland of Culver looms beyond, topped by a tall pillar.

The path leads through bramble thickets, over a footbridge and stile into the last field, keeping along a windbreak of old ash and oak to a stile in the far corner which leads out onto the road leading uphill to St Helens village and downhill to the Duver or harbour bank. (For anyone walking the other way, from St Helens to Seaview, it would be easy to lose the path at the gateway to the Priory Hotel drive and follow the road round, ending up in a holiday centre! Go between the stone gateposts – there is a right of way even though it is not signposted.)

Walk 6: St Helens circular
Distance: 1½ miles (2.4 kilometres)
Map: *see* p.60

St Helens is unique on the island for its nine-acre village green. Buses stop here, and there's plenty of car-parking space, so it is a good starting point for a village walk. Set out seaward along the green, encircled by houses from seventeenth-century thatch to modern neo-Georgian, glimpsing sea and harbour over their roofs. There are cricket and football pitches, and seats, but no geese today – once the flock was so large that the green was known as Goose Island. Halfway along the road on the higher side is a plaque commemorating the birth in 1792 of Sophie Dawes, a smuggler's daughter who became a duchess.

At the end of the grass we walk on downhill, along lower Green Road, to a pair of seats under an oak tree. A path used to turn off here into the woods but at present land subsidence has made the beginning a scramble rather than a walk. However, another entrance has been made a hundred yards further on, onto a pretty little narrow footpath which winds down through the trees, sometimes down steps. Ivy and harts-tongue fern carpet the ground under ash and hawthorn, with garden-escapes montbretia and buddleia.

At the foot of the hill a wooden footbridge leads out onto the Duver, a vast, flat open space of sandy turf between harbour and sea. A detour left across the grass brings us to sand dunes, a row of beach huts and beyond them the Solent's mouth, with a strange sea-mark over on the left, a great slab of whitewashed wall, all that is left of the original church of St Helens, a site founded by St Wilfred in Saxon times; its Norman church was torn away by the sea more than 300 years ago.

The Duver is a fine place to ramble over and of great interest to botanists, who may find autumn squill, evening primrose, the striped trumpets of sea convolvulus and bushes of pale yellow lupin. Returning to the route, we skirt what appears to be part of the harbour but which is in fact a millpond, and soon come to the end of a broad sea wall which divides the sheet of water into two, a lovely walk, though not suitable for small children, since it is unfenced.

Set out along the wall, on your right the old millpond, shining calm, disturbed only by swans or diving tern. On the harbour side small boats and yachts, including Bembridge Red Wings, sail in and out of the narrow harbour mouth. House-boats fringe the far shore, with woods beyond. The wall stretches for nearly a quarter of a mile, turns sharp right and brings you out onto a quay beside an interesting modern house, built on the site of the old tide-mill and using its stones. Passing this, we turn right up a narrow tarmac lane, Mill Road. Pause near the top and look back for a last view of the harbour and hills beyond. This has brought us back to the green, where there are cafés and a pub.

To reach Bembridge, you can in summer catch a small ferry boat from the Duver, near the beach huts; otherwise walk round the harbour, carrying straight on over a stone bridge from the mill house and following the road round. While traffic does whizz past, there is an interesting collection of old barges, houseboats and boatyards to be seen on the harbour side.

Walk 7: Bembridge to Brading
Distance: 3 miles (4.8 kilometres)
Map: *see* p.60

At low tide Bembridge offers vast sandy beaches for walking, with wide views of the Channel and the squat black shape of the Nab tower. A visit to the Maritime Museum in the village will explain its history and also provide an historical background for the next walk, which is across the reclaimed floor of Brading harbour. In the museum a large model explains the various attempts over the years to drain the land, succeeding only in 1878 when the causeway was built where the harbour road now runs.

Take the road from the church in the centre of the village for three-quarters of a mile inland. Where it turns sharply to the left, there is a small car-park. This is also a bus route. From the car-park we turn left down the lane leading to Bembridge Windmill. Nearly forty feet high, built of local stone, three feet thick at the base, with huge sweeps in place and much of the original machinery inside the mill is well worth a visit. The National Trust makes a small admission charge to non-members. Its knoll looks out over a wide, flat expanse of meadows, reclaimed from the sea, rising steeply in the distance to the great headland of Culver Cliff.

Before setting out for Culver or Brading, you may like to visit Steyne Wood, down the green lane straight ahead, leaving the mill on the right, a pleasant green shade in summer where spotted orchids grow tall in the half shade of oak, ash and hazel and the path is fringed with the showy, three-foot stems of drooping sedge.

Back at the mill, turn along behind it, over a stile on the left and down across a field to a gap in a line of oaks. From there you can look down on the canopy of Steyne Wood, especially lovely in spring with its varied tints of new green. Once down the bank, bear right through another hedge gap and follow a rough track downhill, through a gate and diagonally across to the foot of the slope where signposts are visible. This is all farmland, so there are probably cattle and horses – dogs should be on leads.

Once at the signpost we take direction for Brading and step up onto a stone, grass-topped causeway, walking out over land once at the bottom of Brading Haven with a marshy pasture on the right a few feet below us, home of shelduck and curlew, patched here and there with willows. By a pond white with crowfoot in summer we climb a stile – and now be ready to drop flat! A notice warns 'Beware of low-flying aircraft', for all the flat grassland to the left is Bembridge Airport; there are always small aircraft on the ground, usually painted bright colours, so from the distance they look like toys.

We cross a field and another stile on the airfield's outskirts, a fine flowery meadow in summer, with several sorts of clover, purple vetch, forget-me-nots, common orchids, buttercups, sorrel, moon daisies, chickweed and plantains with larks singing overhead. Over another stile into one more meadow, but oh, the difference! Outside airport land now, we are once more back on 'improved' farmland. This field is growing only grass; weed-killer has eradicated the rest, where legend says the Druids once grew mistletoe.

Culver looms higher and higher as we approach its foot. To our left, St Urian's Copse comes into view. The last field is vast, the path winding down the middle, past a lone oak, narrow but still well defined even when through standing corn. Through the trees there is a glimpse of St Helens on rising ground to the north. After skirting the field edge, the path crosses another stile, with thorn thickets on either side, then a stretch of marsh on the left, full of yellow iris and the reeds called 'spires' on the Isle of Wight.

At a signpost we bear right for Brading or detour left to explore St Urian's Copse, a mixed wood of old trees with marshy hollows rich in water-loving plants. Long ago, tradition tells us, this was the site of a great town called Woolverton, but the killing of a pilgrim from Jerusalem brought down a curse, and it was burnt down by the French, never to be restored. (You can walk right through the copse, cross the main road and climb the landward slope of Culver Down, returning to Bembridge by walking seaward along the summit to the cliffs, then turning left and keeping to the cliff-edge path.)

Returning to the main path, we tunnel briefly through trees and then emerge on the spacious harbour floor once again, vast distances all round, silvery willows, mallards quacking, the peep-peep of moorhen scuttling for cover. The path becomes a wide causeway curving round to a fieldgate by a white house. We cross several small bridges over the River Yar or tributary streams where swans often cruise, small boys fish, swallows dip for a drink.

Through the gate a path turns off to the right for St Helens. We keep straight on up Wall Lane, past the ruins of a cement works and some new bungalows, to emerge into Brading High Street between an ancient house and a church.

Here are buses back to Bembridge. If the traffic shooting noisily past is something of a shock after those quiet green miles, rest or picnic in the churchyard where there are various memorial seats.

Brading church, one of the oldest on the island, is well worth a visit, not only for its beauty but to enrich the next walk. In the Oglander Chapel among various memorials to that family lies a full-length effigy of Sir John, complete with moustache, whose memoirs give an unrivalled picture of domestic life in Stuart times and whose home, Nunwell House, we can include in our next walk as it is open on summer afternoons, Sunday to Thursday.

Walk 8: Nunwell Woods circular
Distance: 2 miles (3.2 kilometres)
Map: *see* p.60

After visiting Brading church cross the road and turn up a narrow cut with a one-way sign, then left along West Street – this simply avoids traffic and also passes some pretty thatched cottages. At the Bull Ring, carry on up the hill, Mall Road – there's a seat halfway up. Just beyond, a path on the other side between two houses leads into Nunwell Woods.

Climbing gently between hedges, the path soon opens out past an old overgrown chalkpit where chalk-loving flowers cover the ground, rockrose and thyme, wild carrot, orchids and vetches, and goatsbeard – that golden flower beloved of Henry Williamson, with its great, fragile ball of seeds. All the time you can choose up or down here – narrow tracks lead up onto the bare ridge of Brading Down or down into the woods. We take a path which terraces down through huge old beeches to level ground. A stile is signposted to Nunwell but it is worth carrying on a few hundred yards to find a splendid avenue of lime trees, running down across fields to a glimpse of Nunwell's roofs. (Here a wide track leads up onto the downs, or you can continue on through the woods, a fine, shady route in hot weather, to come out on the Nunwell Farm road.) We walk back to the stile past dark yew trees, ash, oak and modest woodland flowers such as sanicle and enchanter's nightshade, and sit on it for a moment. Far ahead the hills of the mainland undulate across the sky, while nearer lie the red roofs and tall church spires of Ryde.

Down a long field edge, the path leads to a road where a left turn brings us almost at once to the drive winding up to Nunwell House, while to the right the road leads quickly back to Brading. Here we can catch a bus back to Bembridge to pick up the coastal footpath for a fine five-mile cliff walk to Sandown.

Walk 9: Bembridge to Sandown
Distance: 3 miles (4.8 kilometres)
Map: *see* p.60

From the fork near Bembridge church, take the road signposted to Lane End. Here a long jetty leads out to the lifeboat station. From the café and car-park, a path turns south-west along a low grassy cliff, presently fringed with tamarisk and summer chalets, to Forelands. Here too there is a pub, café and car-park: it makes an alternative starting-point if you want to shorten the route by half a mile.

The path continues now along the cliff edge, with an enticing view of Whitecliff Bay ahead, acres of pale sand sheltered under the tall cliffs of Culver, very steep and white, patched here and there with grass. Directly below, willows turn their silvery leaves in the least breeze; in summer the turf is bright with mallow, vetches and sea carrot.

At a T-junction we bear left through a little wood of hazel and fern, then pass the beautifully kept playing-fields of

Bembridge School, the square tower of the chapel making a landmark, to a downhill stretch and a clamouring on the air. In winter it could be gulls – in summer it is children, for we are coming downhill to Whitecliff Bay itself, a big caravan site with cafés and small shops. But the footpath cunningly avoids most of the crowds, passing over the road to the beach on a wooden footbridge, skirting a few summer chalets, climbing now between hedges. All the way this is a very well-defined path with few options for going wrong: where there are turns off, keep along the cliff edge.

A stile brings a complete change of scenery. Ahead lies a white path sloping steeply up the side of a bare down, bright with tiny, chalk-loving plants, such as bird's foot trefoil and thyme. At the top, pause for a moment to look back, for below lies the whole eastern peninsula, the beach curving away in crescents to Lane End, what appear to be toy boats on the far shine of Bembridge harbour, toy planes on the airfield, and the distant Solent with mainland hills beyond.

From the stile you can follow a path going off inland which will curve downhill to the road near to St Urian's Copse, through which you could circle back to the causeway path and return to Bembridge. An unofficial-looking notice on the stile points Sandown to the right, and we do turn inland but only for a few yards before making up hill again to a tall stone finger which has been beckoning from the skyline for miles. This is a memorial to Lord Yarborough, who founded the Yacht Club, the first of its kind, in 1815. On the accession of William IV fifteen years later, this was renamed the Royal Yacht Squadron, whose famous headquarters we shall later pass in Cowes.

Past the memorial we cross to an iron swing gate onto a narrow road. This summit of Culver is broad and almost flat. On it were built several forts and a row of coastguard cottages. Follow the road seaward to explore the ruins of the old fort on the promontory, or landward for the road between Bembridge and Sandown, or wander anywhere over the turf and picnic. There is a restaurant up here too, and cafés.

To walk on toward Sandown, cross the road, and a few yards to the right another metal gate gives access to the fine cliff walk ahead – and all downhill. A slightly sunken path leads down to a gate, but there is no fence on either side! This is a good picnic spot, with a vast view out over Sandown Bay to the headland of Dunnose under Shanklin Downs and blue hills beyond, far away in west Wight. Herring gulls glide across this high territory, screaming at each other, planing down to the sea. The path leads steeply down to a level stretch, and suddenly the terrain is different – from the beach we would have seen white cliffs give way to tawny orange. Redcliff Bay it is called, for here chalk gives way to Wealden clay, a rich hunting-ground for fossil collectors.

The path steepens again downhill and broadens as it comes closer to a large car-park on the outskirts of Sandown. From here you can look back at the sheer white walls of Culver, once climbed by the poet Swinburne who, on crawling exhausted over the summit, came face to face with a startled sheep. Do not be tempted to emulate him though: there are fatal attempts every year.

From the car-park you can catch a bus back to Bembridge or walk along the promenade into Sandown itself, a quarter of a mile. (When the tide is out, there is good shore walking back eastward, with dramatic views of Culver towering up to 500 feet and the possibility of finding fossil fern or dinosaur bones in Redcliff Bay – but don't go beyond it.)

If you are walking on to Sandown, don't miss the Geological Museum above the public library, on the corner as you enter the High Street; its wealth of fossils, from tiny delicate fly wings to chunks of dinosaur vertebra, can lend a whole new dimension to walking the Wight.

III   South-East and South

Walk 1: Sandown to Newchurch
Distance: 3 miles (4.8 kilometres)
Map: *see* p.72

The resort of Sandown lies in a gap of the cliffs with a large hinterland of low-lying marshy country stretching inland along the valley of the Eastern Yar. This provides flat land for two golf courses, and also various quiet walks for those who want to leave behind the crowded ice-cream-and-deckchair scene for a while.

To begin a walk from Sandown to Newchurch and Arreton, go to the top or west end of the High Street, turn up Melville Street, cross over Broadway into Station Road and shortly turn right into Nunwell Street with the station straight ahead – there is usually room to park here. Turn left outside the station yard, through an underpass beneath the line to Shanklin and directly across the road to a footpath through the playing fields to a straight stretch of road, an uninteresting beginning, but pleasant from now on.

Botanists may care to turn in the drive to Fairway Holiday Park, which is also a public footpath, to inspect an overgrown rubbish heap where interesting aliens have been found, including a fine prickly pear with large, showy white trumpets (very poisonous). A narrow, sometimes overgrown footpath turns into a wood just before the caravans begin. Keeping left, this will bring you to the beginning of the marsh path. Less adventurous walkers may follow the road round a

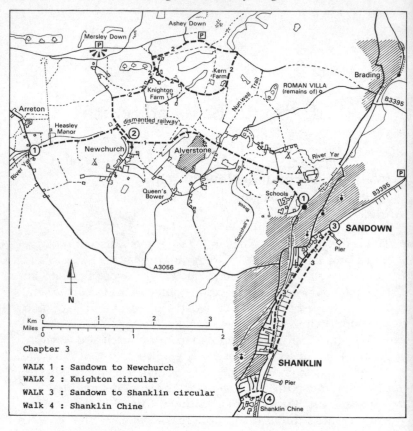

Chapter 3

WALK 1 : Sandown to Newchurch
WALK 2 : Knighton circular
WALK 3 : Sandown to Shanklin circular
Walk 4 : Shanklin Chine

bend by the waterworks and turn off it alongside the river, through a green plain rimmed by Ashey Down.

This wide, firm track follows the old railway line towards Arreton and Newport. Here it is overhung by magnificent tall silvery willows, and passes through thickets of wild flowers, including fragrant meadowsweet, called 'cherry pie' on the island, and showy bright pink wild sweet pea. At a bridge, Scotchells Brook flows into the Yar from the west, the far southern downs visible along its valley. Soon the track narrows to a path and crosses the river on an iron bridge; through thickets of comfrey, pink, purple and cream, it leads along a raised stretch towards a gate onto a road. This is the hamlet of Alverstone.

The railway path continues straight on across the road, but it is more interesting to turn right a few yards to Mill House, where a stile gives onto a path over a footbridge and thence to a delightful stretch right along beside the water, and a riot of water-loving plants, yellow iris, willowherbs, great reed mace and bur reeds, with shy moorhens scooting for cover under overhanging alder and willow, good country for ducks, warblers, even the kingfisher.

Over a stile we come out onto the railway path; again you can follow it to Newchurch through the marsh, but it makes a more varied route to walk straight across it to a plank bridge and stile signposted to Newchurch, which lead to a sloping field often covered in autumn with fairy-ring toadstools. We climb up to a stile at the top into a wood. Here a branch left leads off to Queen's Bower.

The little sandy path winds through oak, birch and bracken with an occasional wild cherry to a more grassy stretch, beautifully rabbit-mown; then another stile leads back into woods sometimes darkened by holly and yew, uphill and presently to gravestones. Here a flight of steps leads up to the churchyard proper of All Saints', Newchurch, which forms a terrace high above the Yar valley with a splendid view, from western downs to eastern cliffs.

The church itself has an unusual wood-clad tower: inside, it is spacious and beautiful, founded by the Normans, with a fourteenth-century rose window in glowing glass and a delightful modern one of St Francis with a friendly wolf. Along the village street, wisteria almost hides the one small general shop. Our way lies down the steep shute beside the church to the river at its foot. Here on the left of the bridge we can pick up the railway again, firm going but with enormous puddles after rain.

Beyond the surrounding marsh, arable fields slope away,

often with crops of sweetcorn taller than a man. Newchurch is surrounded by nurseries and farms, a great place for 'pick your own' vegetables, and in August it holds a Garlic Festival! Look back for a sight of the church perched on its hillock.

A straggle of willow and reed mark the line of the river, providing cover for lapwing and pheasant; in summer the meadows are all a-flicker with swallows and martins hawking for gnats. The track crosses the river, and presently Heaseley Manor comes into view up on the right, a fascinating, rambly house once owned by the monks of Quarr Abbey, who built a great wool room and a mill; later it was owned for 300 years by the Fleming family, who built on Georgian and Victorian extensions. After being split up into labourers' cottages, it fell into ruin, till rescued and lovingly restored. Now it is open to the public.

Our track leads out onto the main Newport to Sandown road. You can cross over and continue walking up the Yar towards Merstone or turn right along the road for a snack at Heaseley, or catch a bus back to Sandown.

Walk 2: Knighton circular
Distance: 2½ miles (4 kilometres)
Map: *see* p.72

Newchurch, close to downs with water-meadows and farmland, has various other walks in the neighbourhood. A circular route, including downs, lanes and fields, begins at the hamlet of Knighton.

Walk down the steep hill from the church, keeping to the right along the lanes, though passing the turn signposted to the sandpits. As the lane begins its climb over the downs, a high and ancient stone wall, moss – and ivy-covered, makes an angle down to the right, where a rushing sound betrays the waterworks and its ponds.

Behind that stone wall once stood Knighton, one of the great houses of the island (pronounced Kay-niton, to distinguish it from Niton on the south coast). Sweet music and the sound of carriage wheels can be heard here every New Year's Eve, it is said, though the house was pulled down in 1820 by Sir Maurice Bisset, who hated the heir, his nephew. Before that it belonged to the Dillington family, whose memorial stones line their chapel in All Saints' Church above.

We pass down beside the wall, by the lodge, bearing right beside a cluster of houses tucked away here and the ruins of some old pumping houses, to a track climbing the flank of a hill. At a cottage entrance this turns sharply right and becomes for a short stretch a sunken lane, green with mossy stones and ferns. At the end a path turns away to Newchurch, but we keep along by a copse of elm and oak and emerge into a large worked-out sandpit, a landscape formerly as bare and cratered as the moon but just being reclaimed by grass, horsetails and mayweed, as well as planted willows. The path is as soft as a beach underfoot, pure sand. On a weekday you will hear diggers working over the hedge on a new stretch – beware of lorries crossing over your path just as it climbs up from the old workings.

A wide track continues on, with a field on one side and a high, thick hedge on the other; this produces crops of giant sloes in autumn and is often the haunt of long-tailed tits. This is a good place to test the hedge theory, which proposes you take a thirty-yard stretch of hedge and count the number of shrubs and trees in it (not scramblers such as ivy and clematis). Each variety means a hundred years in the life of the hedge. Without actually stopping, it was easy to count blackthorn, elder, hawthorn and scrub maple, which makes this hedge some 400 years old – in fact, it may well be more, as we are coming to a very ancient place.

Through a gate the track curves gently uphill, overhung here and there with oak and sycamore, between them glimpses of farmland falling away in gentle folds to woodlands. There are several gates on this walk, each one clearly marked 'Livestock. Please shut gates and keep dogs on lead', and for once it is a pleasure to obey the order because every single gate, though of the heavy metal bar variety, is properly hung and latched. Where one more of them appears to lead into a farmyard, we turn away to the right. The farm is callèd Kern and occupies the site of a medieval village of which no trace remains, a well-chosen location though, facing out to the south under the steep flank of hill to the north. We follow a tarmac drive for a short way, then turn left through another gate, skirting a field dotted with poultry pens. One more long field climb brings us out onto the down itself, chalk country now.

At the top old chalkpits and heaps have long been overgrown by green turf that can be rich in cowslips, mullein and other chalk-loving flowers, but there are often sheep grazing, so little comes to bloom. Bearing left, we reach the top of Ashey Down, quite a steep climb, but for reward there is half the island spread below, miles of quiet, undulating green country stretching away and away to the southern downs and the English Channel.

The last gate appears to lead onto the tarmac road over the downs from Brading to Newport, but we turn at once onto a narrow path, signposted Downlands Way, which runs parallel with the road, with a hedge on either side for a few hundred yards, coming out into a layby where a signpost points down into deep woods, but through the metal wicket gate we turn almost at once along the edge of it, down a path signposted to Knighton. This is steep and often slippery, though there are natural 'steps' of tree roots and chalk ridges. At the foot of the slope we can look up along the vast bulk of the chalk ridge.

Now the path terraces along just above the foot of the down, in and out of a copse line, which divides ploughed field in the valley bottom from downland turf above, then descends a short, steep bank onto a hard farm track. With easier walking underfoot, we can enjoy a wealth of wild flowers in summer, though perhaps autumn is just as lovely, with the flame-pink leaves of spindleberry, dark red of dogwood, crimson haws and scarlet hips, elder with glossy black berries and pink-purple leaves and the silvery fruits of clematis breaking into the pale fluff of old man's beard. Near the end, an old pit is hung with huge old ash trees, leaves turning a vivid yellow.

A gate brings us out onto the tarmac lane. Turning left, we pass a pair of massive stone gate pillars, the ruts between them leading only into a field. Once these were the gates of Knighton. Follow its garden wall along and we are back on the way to Newchurch. Turning right at the gate would bring us up to the main road on the summit of the down.

Walk 3: Sandown to Shanklin circular
Distance: 5 miles (8 kilometres)
Map: *see* p.72

Returning to Sandown to pick up the Coastal Path, we bear inland at the end of the front and climb a footway up the cliff which continues up to Beachfield Road, but we turn off it into Ferncliff, a little tree-hung park formed from an old house and its garden, with a restaurant providing tables on the grass. From here the path keeps to the edge of the cliff, leading first to Battery Gardens, another park but once a fort: you can trace out old arches now covered with Virginia creeper, dry moats, flights of winding steps and old gun-emplacements.

From here, roughly the middle of Sandown Bay, there is a vast view, back to the white walls of Culver Cliff and Sandown itself, the pier thrusting out across acres of flat sand, and forward to Shanklin, with its own pier, sheltered under downs and the headland of cliffs ending in Dunnose, dark cliffs in contrast to Culver. A short stretch of road soon becomes footpath again, shaded by oak trees. (From the road a steep path goes down to the beach.) It soon opens out onto a long stretch of public gardens with seats and flowerbeds. From the cliff edge you can look down onto the vast blue bay which in summer is all zigzagged with bright little craft, red canoes, rainbow wind-surfers, white-sailed yachts.

Where the path does a U-turn you have a close view of the cliff face, dark, sheer and crumbling. Lengths of double fencing show how cliff falls push the path back all the time. Here another path drops to the beach, in three long hairpins: down there the sand is broken up by some two dozen breakwaters into little bays. Rounding a bend, the near view of Shanklin Pier takes one by surprise.

This has been an easy tarmac walk quite suitable for pram-pushers so far, and flat but for a gentle climb up from Sandown. Now, on the outskirts of Shanklin, come the switchbacks, three of them, the last with the deepest plunge, the steepest climb, but it does have a pub in it and several seats on the summit. From here it is downhill all the way. We are above the northern end of Shanklin front, looking directly down onto a children's fun place with Noddy Train and a blow-up castle, and we emerge onto Hope Road.

Various choices offer themselves here. Straight across the road, the cliff path continues, similar in character. Downhill we come to the long promenade, from which you can reach the cliff top again by lift or walk to the far end and turn inland up steep roads to the old part, Shanklin village.

To make a circular walk, turn down Hope Road and left at its foot, past the funfair. This leads onto the sea wall which continues all the way back to Sandown. This is not a narrow wall like the one at Seaview, but wide as a road, making this walk feasible in most states of tide or weather, though it was built not for the walker but as one more effort to protect the cliffs and stop further falls. Actual sand walking is difficult here because of all the breakwaters, earlier attempts to lessen the force of the sea.

Though the view is less spectacular down here, the cliffs themselves are full of interest, orange-brown sandstones and clays of the Lower Green Sand. Along the top and on various ledges grow Hottentot fig, broom and wild tree lupin, while various garden-escapes have colonized the wet slacks at the foot – here is a last stronghold of that magnificent plant, royal fern.

The crumbly nature of the rock makes it ideal for rabbits and voles. Because there is a good food supply, kestrels have colonized the cliffs in recent years, even breeding here. At its northern end the path leads up a slipway onto Sandown esplanade.

Walk 4: Shanklin Chine
Time: Allow 1 hour
Map: *see p.72*

Shanklin's great wooded gorge has been open to the public since 1817 (though there is an entrance fee, and it closes now in winter). Beside the path the stream drops forty feet in a pretty moss – and fern-fringed fall. Trees meet overhead, home of tits and wrens, while grey wagtails frequent the streamside; the moist, shady climate encourages seven kinds of fern, also bamboo, sedge and alder. Further down, where there are pools and more sunlight penetrates the canopy, look for dragonflies. Many twists and turns, bridges and steps bring us to the foot of the chine, and to Fisherman's Cottage right on the shore.

Climbing up again, noticing the Victorian brine bath and the aviary, we return to the small stream which over the years has cut so great a chasm, and cross the footbridge into a deep, sunken road, big old oak and sycamore leaning over it.

Walk 5: Shanklin to Bonchurch and St Boniface
Distance: 2½ miles (4 kilometres)
Map: *see pp.80-1*

From Shanklin we can walk on to Bonchurch by a choice of routes, high and low, but both begin in Shanklin Old Village. From the car-park we cross into the main street, quaint and picturesque, winding between thatched cottages and tea-gardens. A few yards downhill, between the Crab Inn and

Chapter 3

WALK 5 : Shanklin to Bonchurch and St Boniface

WALK 6 : Ventnor to Old Park circular

WALK 7 : Ventnor to Niton

WALK 8 : Niton to Castlehaven circular

WALK 9 : Blackgang to Chale circular

WALK 10: Blackgang to Niton circular

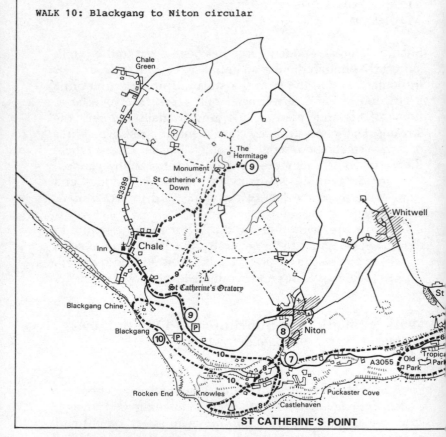

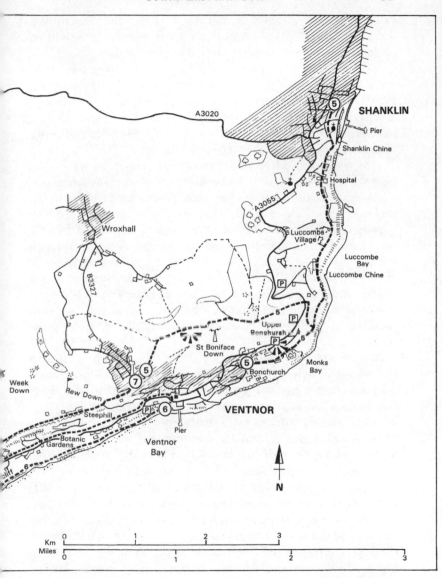

Pencil Cottage, stands a plaque bearing the inscription written for it by the American poet Henry Longfellow, addressed to every walker: 'Traveller, stay thy weary feet.'

Here we turn down a quiet, tree-hung, traffic-free road with a stream running across it and a wooden footbridge. Beside it stands the entrance to Shanklin Chine, which is well worth a detour (*see* p.79, **Walk 4: Shanklin Chine**). Later, moving on into West Wight, we shall discover several more chines – sudden deep clefts in high cliffs.

This leads uphill to a junction of three roads, of which we take the middle one, Luccombe Road, glimpsing the sea as we climb up past the Cottage Hospital till the road tapers away and becomes the cliff path, high above the sea, sheltered by copses and thickets beloved of magpies and jays. Towards the hamlet of Luccombe there are several clearer stretches with a sea view. Luccombe offers cafés, seats and another chine, though it is hardly more than a steep flight of steps down wooded cliffs to the beach – 209 steps! On the long climb back, remember that smugglers used to run up here carrying a couple of barrels of spirit slung over their shoulders.

At the western end of Luccombe the whole cliff top becomes a jungle of hydrangeas, mostly pink, which have escaped from a hydrangea farm and flourished madly. Past there and a house entirely embowered, we come to a parting of ways. The right-hand path leads eventually to the summit of St Boniface Down, but for the moment we will continue walking along the cliff top, though in very different country, for here, down some steps or a slope, we enter the Undercliff.

Long ago a great ledge of rock fell away from the inner cliff, now bowered in old trees, littered with mossy boulders and crossed by small streams. Inland a dark cliff shuts out the world, and the sea murmurs far below. The path winds about through contorted oak, ash and beech, all hung with long ropes of clematis and ivy, a romantic island jungle, before coming out onto open pastures above Monks Bay at Bonchurch. Here a footpath turns down to the shore. We climb up through the fields looking towards a big stone house with lawns terracing the cliff, East Dene, the childhood home of the poet Swinburne. On the left is the tiny old church of Bonchurch, where services are still held in summer.

We come out onto the end of a road, with Winterbourne on the left, where Charles Dickens stayed while writing *David Copperfield*, and massive gate towers on the right, the entrance to East Dene. Following the road, along we come into Bonchurch village, a long tree-hung pond taking up one side, lively with ducks and ornamental waterfowl. At the far end a turn to the left past the church leads down into Ventnor.

Now we return to Luccombe hydrangeas, to try the higher route which is the official Coastal Path, certainly further from the sea, but bypassing Ventnor town. At the railings, go up the steep flight of steps on the right, and a short climb brings you out onto a grassy picnic area with benches and tables. Above this lie a small car-park and the main coast road. Cross this and mount the stile opposite. The way ahead is a very steep climb straight up the face of the down, short turf rabbit-mown and studded in summer with all the small chalk-loving carpet-flowers such as thyme, eyebright, felworts, dwarf and carline thistles, with taller scabious and knapweed here dwarfed by the sea wind. Hawthorn flourishes on the lower slopes, so much so that the National Trust, who own the land, have cleared clumps which threatened to become impassable thickets.

Pause at the stile and turn round to enjoy a vast view right out over the English Channel, Sandown Bay and eastern Wight.

Over the stile the climb continues but gradually levelling out: late summer brings a brilliant display of rosebay willowherb here. Other flowers bring a surprise – heather, bracken, all the signs of acid soil suddenly. This means we have reached the summit cap of gravel. Look ahead and there is a less welcome surprise, a Thing, metal, monstrous and whirling round, a rectangular radar dish in action. The path skirts along westward beside the radar emplacement, the slate roofs of Ventnor on its steep terraces slowly coming into view far below, with the Western Channel, and on the right appears a deep fold in the downs in which the railway used to run. The path downhill is very steep here and comes out into what used to be the station yard walled in by the downs; now it is a small industrial estate.

We have to take to the road here for a short stretch and decide once again whether to proceed westward on the upper or lower cliff. St Boniface itself is a huge down, well worth exploring further, but its flanks around Ventnor are so steep that it is pleasanter to set out from Wroxall – *see* p.125. There is a cheat way too – you can actually *drive* onto the top.

Walk 6: Ventnor to Old Park circular
Distance: 5 miles (8 kilometres)
Map: *see* pp.80-1

The Undercliff walk begins at the south-western end of Ventnor sea front, climbing gently up through a park with grass seats and flowerbeds. Where the cliff has fallen away, substantial wooden footbridges cross the gaps, giving a sight of the bare white face – elsewhere it is clothed with samphire, wild stock and trefoils, dropping to a shore which is one huge jumble of rocks. A plaque commemorates the end of coastal protection work in Castle Cave below. This is dated 1984, but already many of the great concrete blocks have been flung out of alignment by the battering waves.

Soon after, the park ends, wild hedges edge the path and a branch to the left down rough steps leads to Steephill Cove, a tiny rocky bay with a few cottages tucked under the low, bushy cliffs, protected by a wide rock sea wall. Small boats lie about on the smooth sand between the reefs, with lobster pots and nets drying. A cormorant hangs his wings out to air on the breakwater, and herring gulls clamour on the wall. Tucked between tree mallows and the cliff are several small Victorian bathing huts, still in use. In summer there are boat trips and fresh lobster salads in the small café. Steephill is really tucked away from the world, sheltered to the west by a small headland, its strata tilted on end.

By the café a path climbs steeply up to rejoin the one along the cliffs which soon leads between hedges to the Botanic Gardens. We can carry straight on above the sea, but the gardens are well worth a detour.

Ventnor reached its Victorian heyday as a health resort with the building of an immense chest hospital, its gardens laid out by the patients themselves as part of their cure. When the building was pulled down, the grounds were transformed into Steephill Botanic Gardens and planted with many exotic species which flourish in this peculiarly sheltered place, the high inner cliff walling off north winds. Turn inland at the signpost to the gardens and walk downhill to a path which runs right through the gardens, parallel with the cliff. Camellias clothe the old walls, figs and bananas ripen, roses bloom most of the year round a pool near the pub, café and Smugglers Museum. There are rock gardens, bright with tiny flowers, and huge old palm trees from the original planting.

At the far end we turn left up a grassy slope which leads back to the cliff edge. From time to time this rears up with small hillocks, rather like the Pembroke coast, their slopes natural rock gardens of thyme and bird's foot trefoil, sea campion and sea-pink. A few of the small coves are accessible by steps or a scramble, a splendid place for fossil-hunting, though the beaches themselves are mostly pebble and rock. Orchard's Bay lies directly below Lisle Combe, home of the late poet Alfred Noyes, whose book *The Incompleat Gardener* is a magical description of all this coast. Crossing a stream, we come down onto firm sand, strewn with chunks of masonry the size of buses.

In 1883 William Spindler conceived the grand scheme of building a new town and harbour here, but the sea soon disposed of his harbour wall, and the idea was abandoned, like these great chunks known locally as Spindler's Folly. A pity it is not possible to walk further along the cliffs, which beyond the cove have fallen away into a morass of mud, crevasses and bramble – which is why the official Coastal Path follows the inner cliff top. But by the stream outfall we can climb some steps and turn inland towards Old Park.

Keeping right, up through the woods, we meet its boundary wall and, keeping alongside, soon come in sight of the house, now an hotel. This land was one of the medieval hunting parks, with a charter issued in 1309 for hawking. Old stone farm buildings have been converted into a glass-blowing studio, where you can watch craftsmen at work, while the land round an ornamental lake has been transformed into a tropical bird garden. Turning left past the glass studio and right onto the drive, we climb up to road-level through the wood edge, pursued by strange cries of peacocks, cockatoos and macaw.

Coming out onto wide tarmac, there are several choices. We can turn straight up the hill to the Undercliff Road and the St Lawrence Inn, where there are buses back to Ventnor, or walk straight ahead up a narrower road, a pleasanter route, to reach the road further east and visit St Lawrence Church with its Pre-Raphaelite stained glass, or turn right, down a steep little footpath which leads back onto the cliffs and return to Ventnor.

Walk 7: Ventnor to Niton
Distance: 4½ miles (7.2 kilometres)
Map: *see* pp.80-1

The official Coastal Path to Niton begins in the Whitwell Road, Ventnor, where a signpost points through the seaward hedge and leads onto a path running between thick hedges parallel with the road. (Beside the sports stadium tucked in a fold of downs at Watcombe Bottom, a fine ridge walk begins, the Stenbury Trail, leading over to Wroxall and eventually to Newport *see* p.49.) Soon a path branches downhill to the Undercliff Drive, but we keep straight on, with downs rising all round inland, and tantalizing glimpses of the sea, far below, between ash and thorn. Where the path veers away from road, the trees thin enough to show that we have been all this time walking along the extreme edge of a high, sheer cliff which plunges to the Undercliff below, where its foot is lost in woodland.

Where steps lead down to another Undercliff path, it is worth descending a little way to study the cliff face, its pale stone colonized here and there by ivy and fern, and sheer as a wall. Back on the top, enclosing hedges and a swerve to the right bring us to a stile and very steep steps down into a sunken lane, St Lawrence Shute – before the Undercliff drive was built, this was the only way to reach the village. You may like to detour down the road to see the old church of St Lawrence, dating from Norman times and claiming to be the smallest church in England till it was enlarged in the last century.

The Coastal Path continues straight across the Shute, with a steep flight of steps up the bank to a double stile at the top. We follow the hedge back to the cliff edge – where it dies away, so for several fields to come there is a clear view right out over the great wooded ledge below to the sea cliffs scalloped into many small coves, and eastward to Ventnor and its pier. Topping a rise, the western view begins to open out, the highest point called High Hat. When some wireless masts and a house come into view, we are walking over the tunnel which once held the railway line between Newport and Ventnor.

Later, the Cripple Path winds up the cliff face to meet our summit way. Tradition says this was the way the lame and sick came, on pilgrimage to the White Well, a spring from which the nearby village of Whitwell derives its name. Perhaps it was not always so steep; today only the really fit would want to cope with the Cripple Path!

For most of its length this is a splendid, airy walk, with vast views of coastline and sea and many half-hidden coves ideal for smugglers. From this high vantage-point you get some idea of the problems confronting the Revenue officers, even if they did know a cargo was to be landed along this stretch of coast. Niton was a centre of smuggling: three out of four families engaged in 'the night trade', from the squire downwards.

The path continues to skirt between cliff edge and several fields till we come nearer Niton, where it becomes walled with blackthorn, meets an old stone wall and swings inland. A path leading off on the left hand leads down to the Undercliff road, and a little further on is signposted on the opposite side to Whitwell. We follow the stone wall round to meet the main road.

This is Barrack Shute, which joins the two halves of the village. Turn right up the hill for the shops and church clustered round the crossroads. To continue on the Coastal Path, cross the road and, a few yards higher up, turn down Boxers Lane. For the Undercliff and lower Niton we turn down the hill. There is a pub in each half of the village, locally called Crab-Niton to distinguish it from Knighton inland. An island name for a stream is 'buddle', and here by a stream on the lowest road in lower Niton is the Buddle Inn, a good place for pub food, with a garden looking straight out to sea.

Walk 8: Niton to Castlehaven circular
Distance: 2 miles (3.2 kilometres)
Map; *see* pp.80-1

The Buddle Inn is the starting-point for a circular walk to St Catherine's Lighthouse and back. Go some 200 yards westward along the road; where it turns away inland, carry straight on downhill, a narrowing, leafy way with a National Trust sign at the foot saying 'Knowles Farm'. Then it turns towards the sea, the trees fall back, you round a corner, and with dramatic suddenness the lighthouse appears below, the tower tiered above closely grouped houses and all pristine white, like a wedding cake. The tower was once much higher, the light frequently shrouded in Channel fog, so it was lowered some thirty feet.

Inland the wall of cliff has been replaced by more gently rising hummocks and hillocks outcropped with huge rocks and patched with thorn. Past the white outer walls of St Catherine's Lighthouse, we walk on down to Knowles Farm, a compact group of grey stone buildings, now used as summer cottages, the land all round criss-crossed with stone walls. Through the old farmyard and over a stile we turn down toward the sea and can soon glimpse a rock-strewn shore beneath low cliffs. St Catherine's Point has an atmosphere different from that of any other part of the island: stone walls and wild shore recall Cornwall. In summer mood this is a lovely picnic spot – you can wander on to the next small headland, Rocken End.

We reach the cliff edge, cross a stile and at once some steps in the wall to a path inside the perimeter of the lighthouse grounds, sheltered by the walls and bushes of tamarisk. Broken walls at the side are *not* relics of a Roman lighthouse, as visitors are often told, but a reminder of days when cottagers needed to be self-sufficient – in fact, pigsties! Here we pass the light tower very close and will be blasted out of the ground if the foghorn is suddenly needed. Steps lead down onto the cliff, with huge rocks visible on the beach below.

The cliff is still low but constantly outcrops into bare rock, a splendid place for flowers in summer: samphire, sea-pinks, rock spurrey, wallflowers gone wild and a rare stock all form natural rock gardens. Eastward the cliffs grow taller, darker, while out to sea, white, broken water betrays St Catherine's Race.

A kissing-gate leads onto a small caravan site. Halfway across we turn inland into a yard and turn right to reach the sea. In a few yards we are in the bay called Castlehaven: an old cottage, a little green with a seat in the middle, boathouses, small boats and their tackle strewn about, gulls crying, clouds of spray as waves break on black rocks.

Turning back, it is a long, slow climb uphill between banks of reed, bracken and thorn. Soon after a hairpin bend a flight of steps goes up on the left, leading out opposite the Buddle Inn, close beside the real Buddle, dropping down the bank in a series of cascades half hidden in horsetails. The longer but less punishing way is to continue on up Castlehaven Lane. The old name for the cove below was Reeth Bay, said to derive from 'wraith' (ghost) from the number of drowned sailors washed onto its beaches. The newer name derives from a large earthwork on the cliffs, known as the Old Castle.

A last climb brings us up to road-level. (Further along, a path leads at first along a house drive, towards the next cove east, Puckaster, where Charles II landed in 1675, after a great storm in the Channel.) To reach the Buddle we turn left a few hundred yards along the road.

Walk 9: Blackgang to Chale circular
Distance: 4 miles (6.4 kilometres)
Map: *see* pp.80-1

The viewpoint car-park or bus stop above Blackgang, the next village westward, makes a good starting-point for several walks. For St Catherine's Down, cross the road, mount a flight of steps and climb a stile marked HT with a yellow flash and the silhouette of a stone turret which can actually be seen on the skyline above. The path turns left, skirting a field along the contour of the hill round hollows filled with foxgloves, with a vast view out over west Wight, red-brown cliffs below rising to the far white walls of Freshwater, with the Needles Rocks and beyond again to the distant coast of Dorset.

The path veers inland, uphill over several stiles onto downland proper, the turf bright in summer with bird's foot trefoil, clover, thyme and big clumps of thistle beloved of butterflies and a whole chorus of larks. Over on the right is a radio mast attached to a round, squat building. One more stile and we are on the summit, commanding a view reminiscent of that song, "On a clear day you can see for ever and ever and ever" – from Culver Cliff in east Wight, west to Dorset, south far out over the English Channel.

Here stands that turret, more properly an octagonal stone tower with pointed roof, all that remains of St Catherine's Oratory. In 1314 Walter de Godeton stole wine from a ship wrecked in Chale Bay and destined for a priory; as penance he built the oratory, with a priest to say masses and to keep a light burning at night to warn ships off this deadly coast. Go inside the tower, where it is square, and look up at the eight windows, the sootmarks of ancient fires. Long after Henry VIII extinguished light and oratory, and after many terrible wrecks in Chale Bay, including that of the *Clarendon*, Trinity House built another lighthouse here, whose remains are that squat building to the west. Though it panicked the local cows, it was of limited use because so often wrapped in fog.

Continuing north from the tower, a vast spread of north Wight comes into view, dipping into the shallow valley of the River Medina. The path goes downhill beside a fence, looking down on the long lower ridge ahead. At the foot of the slope we veer to the left, then through a gateway onto the lower ridge, a lovely, airy walk winding through gorse and foxgloves to the Hoy Monument, a tall stone pillar surmounted by a ball, erected by Mr Hoy in 1814 to commemorate the visit of Tsar Alexander I; much later a plaque was added, with neat irony, in memory of men killed fighting the Russians in the Crimean War.

From here you can continue on down the side of the hill, turning left at the road to reach Chale Green and buses or return the same way, or return part way then circle back via Chale church. For this route, when near the oratory again, look for a small radar dish down on the right and walk towards it. Turn right from this old marlpit site to a waymarked gate and a track leading down the valley, through a field to a farm road and some fine farm buildings including a tithe barn. This is called Chale Abbey Farm, though there never was an abbey here – on old documents it appears as Chale Anney. We turn left along the road, passing the Clarendon Hotel, built partly of timber from that wreck, and the church. In the table tombs of the old churchyard, smugglers used to hide their barrels and even sometimes themselves!

At the T-junction with the coast road we cross over and go down the lane named 'The Terrace'. It is worth walking a few hundred yards to its end, for it breaks off jaggedly a little further inland each year as the high cliff falls away. A narrow footpath near the beginning of the lane leads up to Blackgang, avoiding the road. A seat halfway up, bowered in evergreen oak, looks straight out over a green field to the sea. This path emerges where the road branches to Blackgang, the viewpoint visible above.

Walk 10: Blackgang to Niton circular
Distance: 4½ miles (7.2 kilometres)
Map: *see* pp.80-1

A fine circular coastal walk also begins at the View Point, involving some rough going and possibly scrambling for a short stretch. This follows the line of the old coast road to Niton and returns along the cliff top.

We climb a stile near the car-park entrance and follow a grass path downhill, facing a magical view right out across the south-west coast to the Needles, then over another stile with a yellow flash along a little valley newly planted with sycamore, to a large car-park. Crossing this, heading for the towering figure of a smuggler complete with barrel on shoulder, we reach the hamlet of Blackgang with its famous chine.

Opened to the public as long ago as 1843, a guide-book of the time describes it as 'a black and sombre chasm five hundred feet deep where dark waters flow'. Today it is a Fantasy Theme Park, much of it aimed at children, but the traditionally built wooden sawmill powered by a waterwheel gives a real glimpse of old island village trades such as bodger, cooper and wheelwright, while the museum should not be missed by anyone contemplating the wonderful coast walk westward.

The wooden building was built over the skeleton of a whale, but its chief fascination is in the collection of wreck pictures which hang round the walls, for Chale Bay below was long known as 'The Graveyard' for its terrible currents and hidden reefs.

Continuing our walk, we set off eastwards down the narrow tarmac road with a few houses on the seaward side – until it disappears. In 1838, when the Undercliff Drive was becoming fashionable, a continuation of it was built, terracing along the cliffs to Blackgang, but the middle section was destroyed in 1928 by a huge landslide. 'The whole cliff face became detached and swayed forward, then thundered down on to the road below,' said the newspaper report. Another fall in 1973 further shortened the tarmac stretch, so only a rough trail leads ahead now, degenerating into a narrow path as we reach the site of the original fall.

The land drops away in a steep terrace of grass and copse and pool to the tawny shingle beach far below, while high above towers the inner wall, Gore Cliff, jackdaws and rock doves circling its sheer face. Every winter minor falls modify the path across but it is an enchanting place in summer, a wilderness of mossy rocks and little streams, thickets of buddleia and thorn, green with horsetails and willowherbs. Take whatever winding path has been trodden out this year and discover grassy patches ideal for picnics, or a bush full of butterflies or a basking lizard, all against the background of the Channel spread far below. At the eastern end, a steep scramble leads up to the Niton end of the old road and a small car-park.

The lane. easy walking now, slopes gently down between stone walls past hanging woods falling to the sea, full of the peaceful croo-croos of wood pigeons, to a junction with Sandrock Road on the outskirts of Niton. (Downhill brings us to the lighthouse.) Turning uphill, we pass the blackened rafters and gables of Sandrock Springs, a picturesque house destroyed by fire. The spring itself was once much visited for its supposed health-giving properties; the church register mentions a ship wrecked 'beneath the Sandrock Spring Dispensary'.

The road comes out onto the main Undercliff Road from Ventnor, here called Barrack Shute, since soldiers were stationed here in Napoleon's time for fear of invasion from across the Channel. About 300 yards up the steep hill we turn left into Boxer's Lane, signposted to Blackgang, past a few houses. Then it becomes a pretty, tree-hung track climbing between a stone wall hardly visible beneath moss and ferns, and a high bank where badger paths thread through the ivy. The going is quite steep and rough till we come to a stile at the top and out onto a level field – the cliff top, in fact, though the edge is screened by trees, with the green slopes of St Catherine's Down opening out on the right.

Here the path is less plain, but we simply keep along the cliff edge to the next stile and the next. Soon trees fall away and we follow a path with field fence on one side, while on the other Gore Cliff plunges down toward our earlier route. For those who don't mind heights, this is a wonderful open stretch, looking down on treetops and wheeling gulls far below.

Near at hand the cliff edge becomes a veritable rock garden in summer, hung with papery white flowers of sea-campion, bright sea-pinks, dusky sea-carrot and glaucous samphire. Eventually we reach a seat overlooking the roofs and trees of Blackgang, and here the path turns inland for a short way, bringing us down steps into the car-park.

The stretch from St Lawrence to the Needles and round to Totland has recently been designated 'Tennyson Heritage Coast'. A display panel in the car-park shows a map of the footpaths round about, and a geological diagram showing the strata to be found westward and explaining how the land ahead has assumed its shape.

IV   Newport and the North

Walk 1: Newport Town Trail
Time: Allow 1 hour
Map: *see* p.96

Newport, the capital of the island, lies in a hollow on the highest navigable stretch of the River Medina, centrally situated with buses radiating out to every corner of the island.

It became the capital after the decline of Newtown, though Sir John Oglander of Nunwell wrote of it, 'Newport was a very poor town, the houses mostly thatched, the streets unpaved. The Bailiffs themselves were but fishermen and oyster-draggers.' That was in the seventeenth century: in the next it began to prosper. Two hundred wagons of grain would converge on the town on a Tuesday, market day, some to be 'exported' – that is, sent to the mainland from the busy quays, and the town was renowned for its pretty girls. Prosperity brought the building of more elegant town houses. Above today's shop fronts are many fine Georgian features.

Now even the beast market has gone, but rows of stalls every Tuesday and Friday help the town retain its homely, market atmosphere, and a walk round it reveals much of interest.

From the bus station we use the panda crossing and continue into St James's Square. In its heyday, the three open spaces in Newport each played a part on market day. St James's Square was originally the beast market – older

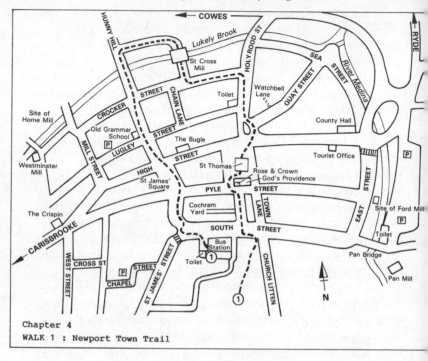

Chapter 4
WALK 1 : Newport Town Trail

residents still refer to it as 'the market'. At the north end stands a memorial to Queen Victoria, and near it a much newer one, a bronze bust of Earl Mountbatten, Governor of the Isle of Wight till his murder in Ireland.

Crossing the High Street into Lower St James's Street, we soon come to the Old Grammar School on the corner of Lugley Street, a fine early seventeenth-century building where Charles I, then a prisoner in Carisbrooke Castle, came to sign the Treaty of Newport. Downhill the road leads to a bridge over the Lukely Brook, which was once the northern gateway into the town. A boarded-up building to the left of the bridge was once Town Gate Mill, later used as assembly rooms for local balls.

Crossing the road, we walk round the gable end of Red

Cross House, signposted to Crocker Street, under the broken-off walls of a railway viaduct once carrying trains to Freshwater, to the stream bank. This little trickle of water was utilized to turn millwheels right down through Carisbrooke and into the town. Here it falls through a sluice underneath yet another, St Cross Mill. The path turns through the buildings, up a narrow cobbled alley. Look up and you can see its name-plate still in position. We walk straight ahead, up St Cross Lane into Crocker Street. The name St Cross comes from a priory, founded here by the stream in 1120.

Having turned the millwheel, the waters of Lukely Brook were immediately put to use by the brewery, both for making beer and for floating barrels away in barges. Turning left along Crocker Street, we pass the old brewery buildings which have elegant wrought-iron grilles over the windows. On the other side of the road stands a house built about 1580, thought to be the oldest in the town.

The T-junction brings us to Holyrood Street. Turning right and crossing over, we come to a narrow cut between houses crossed high up by an enclosed bridge. Look up and just beneath it you can see a great bell hanging. Watchbell Lane has recently taken on a new lease of life, with a row of charming little boutiques selling china, antiques and clothes: it brings us out into a space beside the pillared town hall, which used to be the dairy market.

Cross to the far side of the High Street and into St Thomas's Square, which is largely taken up by the church itself. An older building was burned down; this is Victorian. Whatever else you see in Newport, don't fail to visit the beautiful, moving tomb of a royal princess inside St Thomas's. Princess Elizabeth was the fourth child of Charles I. After his execution she was sent to Carisbrooke Castle and died there, aged fifteen, but her coffin lay in an unmarked grave till Queen Victoria ordered the present memorial in the north-east corner of the church, a pale little full-length figure inside broken bars. There is also a fine full-length effigy of Sir Edward Horsey, who used to dance to the foot of Arreton

Down with his mistress, Dowsabel Mill of Haseley Manor.

The Rose and Crown pub beside the church recalls the story of a young girl who ran out of the crowd to present King Charles I with a rose when he was being escorted through Newport. Behind it, a little way east, stands God's Providence House with a beautiful eighteenth-century shell porch, but its name comes from an older house on the same site where it is said the plague stopped after its virulent outbreak in 1584. Turn up the cut beside it, and Town Lane brings us back to South Street and the bus station, but we will cross the street and go straight on to end our walk in the park.

The pavement leads through a massive Tudor gateway into a green oasis full of mature trees with seats scattered about and a formal rose garden in one corner. In the Middle Ages this was the butts, where archery was practised, but the outbreak of plague was so severe that the field was taken over as a burial ground and used as such until the nineteenth century – a few gravestones remain, notably the memorial to Valentine Gray, a chimney-sweep's boy.

Walk 2: Newport to Whippingham church
Distance: 3 miles (4.8 kilometres)
Map: *see* p.99

Since Newport *was* originally a port, some of the most interesting buildings are those in the old trading quarter near the River Medina, which we can visit *en route* to river-bank walks.

Returning to the town hall, with its conspicuous clocktower, we bear left down Quay Street, a wide thoroughfare still lined with Georgian and even older houses built by rich merchants, though many are now offices. At its foot we carry straight on to the quays themselves; there are seats here for watching the river traffic of swans, small boats and the occasional cargo ship. As we set out down the east bank to walk to Folly, it is necessary to keep a sharp eye out

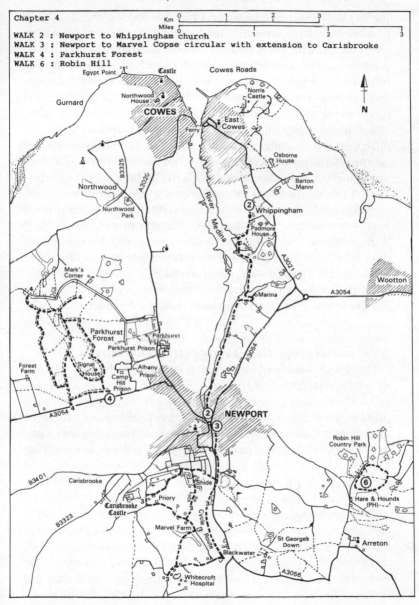

Chapter 4

WALK 2 : Newport to Whippingham church
WALK 3 : Newport to Marvel Copse circular with extension to Carisbrooke
WALK 4 : Parkhurst Forest
WALK 6 : Robin Hill

for lorries, swinging cranes and fork-lift trucks, for this is still a working port, bringing in building materials, exporting grain. Soon after, warehouses block our view of the river, though we can turn off onto a narrow grass footpath running beside the road but just above it. This skirts Seaclose recreation ground and brings us out right beside the river, the road having come to an end.

Beyond the playing-fields, the path winds in and out of old oaks and willows above muddy beaches where grey mats of sea-purslane grow, with sea-beet, the white stars of scurvy grass and tall sea-aster. Hazel or thorn hedges cut off the river from time to time but it opens out again along one more playing-field, revealing a small boatyard opposite, and a skyline of dark trees in the distance, the pines of Parkhurst Forest. Then the bank is broken by several creeklets, a delightful part of the walk, little footbridges leading between thickets of wild roses – or shining rose hips in autumn.

Where the path mounts a causeway, we are walking between the river and the millpond of East Medina Mill, destroyed in a spectacular fire in 1945. Look back up the river for a unique view of Newport, the tower of St Thomas's seeming just to reach the height of the downs beyond.

Hardly a vestige of mill remains; instead, beached inside the millpond is a paddle-steamer with tall red-and-black funnels, the *Ryde Queen*, now used as a clubhouse. Across the quay rear the tall masts of an old Baltic trader, now called the *Pirate Ship*, a restaurant. Here an arm of the river has been turned into a large marina, from which a rough lane leads up to the main Newport to Ryde road (it is *very* rough, not recommended for car-proud drivers; less serious for walkers, who can avoid the enormous potholes).

To move on down river we keep to its edge and cross a catwalk over the lock gates into fields. Opposite you can see the spire of Northwood church pointing above the trees. Here the river widens out, a splendid stretch for bird-watching. From the path which closely follows the bank, you may see black-and-white oyster-catchers, redshank, little grebe diving, a solitary, motionless heron fishing, groups of dunlin and ringed plover casing the shoreline – more birds probably if the tide is out, as they feed on the mudbanks.

Up ahead a curve of the river hides the sea, though it is close; the view is of the wharves, chimneys and masts of East Cowes. This is presently shut off by enclosing hedges, where it is often muddy, emerging again onto open grass strewn with boats, tackle and rope and ending at the Folly Inn, whose history began some 300 years ago when a sloop ran aground here: the captain built on a room and settled down. Sick horses used to be brought down for a certain cure – a gallon of warm ale. Today it has a name for good food and a terrace looking right out over the river.

Industrial buildings now occupy the bank, so we turn inland up the lane for some 200 yards. Where it swerves round to the right and the tall fence ends, we take an inconspicuous path to the left: there is a footpath sign but it is not visible from the lane. This leads through an oak wood to a stile into a meadow which offers a first glimpse of Whippingham church tower. The path strikes across the middle of the field uphill, then down to a stile-footbridge combination peculiar to these parts and to another small oak wood, fringing a stream running down to the river and bright with bluebells in spring – you can detour along it, by a streamside path. The way ahead passes through another field, cutting across the corner to a stile in the top hedge under the tallest oak tree. From here we can look back to the river full of small boats at anchor and the compact huddle of farm cottages and church on the opposite bank, which is the old village of Northwood.

A last stile leads onto a narrow path beside the stone wall of Whippingham churchyard, emerging into the road opposite a striking row of terracotta-coloured almshouses erected by Queen Victoria for her retainers at Osborne. Whippingham church was designed by Prince Albert with a splendid five-pinnacled tower, reminiscent of a castle on the Rhine. Inside, a great octagonal lantern lights the central crossing;

there are many memorials to Victorian royalty and a beautiful bronze screen.

The lane leads uphill, past a tiny shop called the Refectory and Padmore House, an old farm enlarged in Queen Anne style and now a hotel with fine river views. A tunnel is said to lead from it down to the Folly Inn, doubtless dating from smuggling days. The lane comes out onto the main road beside the bus stops for Newport and East Cowes. Nearby are Barton Manor, Osborne House and Norris Castle, all with beautiful grounds to explore.

Walk 3: Newport to Marvel Copse circular, with an extension to Carisbrooke
Distance: 4 miles (6.4 kilometres) or 5 miles (8 kilometres) if extended to Carisbrooke
Map: *see* p.99

The next walk explores the southern outskirts of Newport. Though the town has thrown out long brick tentacles in all directions, it is still possible to reach green fields very quickly, as in the walk to Whippingham.

Starting from the bus station, we go up through Litten Park to Medina Avenue and turn left along it, keeping straight along the new bypass to a metal railed bridge, below which the River Medina flows down a series of steps and curves away towards the quay. Cross the busy road with care, go down a gravel path to the river bank – and the town disappears. There are a few house backs and gardens, the traffic can still be heard, but we are on a narrow path winding through tall grass, under sycamore and alder, beside the stream, presently branching left over a wooden bridge. Garden-escapes such as Michaelmas daisies and montbretia flourish among thistles and yellow iris.

When the path becomes more open, it is easier to glimpse mallard or a moorhen scooting for cover under the willows. Where a wooden footbridge with railings crosses the stream, leading to Shide, we turn away from it and follow a tall wooden fence round to a road but, crossing straight over, find the path continues along by the stream only on the other side, signposted to Blackwater. Here the water is held back by a small weir where black-headed gulls often come to bathe. Soon river and path are divided by small fields and tall, water-loving crack willows and alders, with lady fern flourishing beneath them. We are in open country now, a green ridge ahead crowned with pines; near at hand various interesting plants grow in their season, including the scarce hemp-nettle, flax and purple loosestrife.

Reaching Blackwater, we leave the old railway line to Sandown, whose route we have been following, and turn right up a narrow, tree-hung lane especially pretty in spring when the many wild cherries are in bloom, and in autumn when their leaves turn shades of crimson.

Reaching the entrance to Whitecroft Hospital, we turn along a footpath opposite its entrance which arrows through fields, straight and sandy underfoot with open views north and west to Carisbrooke Castle and the hills above Gatcombe, climbing gently till it turns downhill into Marvel Copse, sloping north with high sandy banks, old oaks and more fine cherry trees. Small paths go off here and there waiting to be explored, but the main track veers round eastward and beside a solitary cottage turns into a narrow footpath skirting its garden. (There is no right of way past the front of the cottage.) This path, trapped between high banks and facing north, can be very wet and muddy, even in summer, but it quickly leads onto narrow tarmac, Marvel Lane, and a whole choice of routes.

The quickest way back to Newport is to turn left along the lane and follow it uphill past the nursery, then downhill where it turns into Watergate Road to a small roundabout and straight on to the next crossroads, where Litten Park is a few yards away on the right.

To extend the walk to Carisbrooke, from Marvel Lane almost immediately turn left again into Nunnery Lane.

Follow this westward till it eventually passes under the high grey stone walls of St Dominic's Priory, locally known as 'The Nunnery', and the Whitcombe Road. Opposite is a car-park overlooking Carisbrooke Castle. Turn down the hill a few hundred yards, then up a long flight of steps climbing the bank which leads to the footpath over Mount Joy, said to be anciently named after the god Jove, making a pair with the hill to the east named after Pan. The path skirts a large cemetery, but the view beyond is superb, right across Newport and the Medina valley to the Solent and mainland beyond. We descend into Whitepit Lane and turn right to the small roundabout previously mentioned.

Walk 4: Parkhurst Forest
Distance: 1¼ miles (2 kilometres) or 2½ miles (4 kilometres) or ramble
Map: *see* p.99

Just outside Newport stretch nearly 1200 green acres of Parkhurst Forest, remnant of the forest and royal park that once stretched right across north Wight. During the Napoleonic Wars much timber was felled for shipbuilding, but afterwards the northern slopes were replanted with oaks. The Forestry Commission took it over in 1928. In the southern part there are long stretches of pine and fir, though various ornamental species have been planted beside the rides.

The Forestry Commission have laid out a picnic site, and there is a car-park right in the woods. A map sets out two routes for walkers, or one can just wander about the grass rides and gravel tracks. The shorter track, waymarked in blue, is 1¼ miles long, leading through the southern and mostly conifer plantations, one of the most likely places to see red squirrels. Sit down and listen – you may well hear the scritch-scratch of their claws on the bark as a clue to their whereabouts, and the 'laugh' of a woodpecker or the harsher cries of jay or magpie. Where cross rides make gaps, a framed view appears of flat fields below, rising to the western downs.

The longer walk, waymarked in green and 2½ miles long, circles round into the northern woods where the oaks are now around 150 years old. Along the sunnier rides wild flowers flourish on the verges, with comfrey in several colours along the ditches. Some young oak has been planted but much of the clay soil is poor, suitable only for conifers. A gravel track winds through from the entrance in Forest Road to Marks Corner on the northern side.

The forest is large enough to wander about in all day – it is quite possible to get lost, if you are not following a trail, so take a compass if you prefer to make your own way. The gravel tracks provide firm walking in winter, the grass paths summer shade.

For the energetic there is a Wayfaring Course; for the rest, seats at intervals. Brimstone and other butterflies flit along the rides, wood ants build tall castles, adders and lizards come out to bask in the sun.

Walk 5: Cowes Town Trail
Time: Allow 1½ hours
Map: *see* p.106

Cowes stands on the northern tip of the island, its narrow High Street winding between sea and hill, another homely little town except in 'The Week', when it becomes the yachting centre of the world, starting-point for the Fastnet Race, the Powerboat Race and, of course, the local events. All the year round it looks toward the sea, with many yacht clubs, boatbuilding yards and ferry landings.

Cowes began as a mere fishing village, growing into a town only when Henry VIII ordered the building of two castles to defend either bank of the River Medina; these were called the East Cowe and the West Cowe, hence the name. The East Cowe has disappeared. Later, smugglers had fast boats built in its shipyards – Customs and Excise followed suit. At John

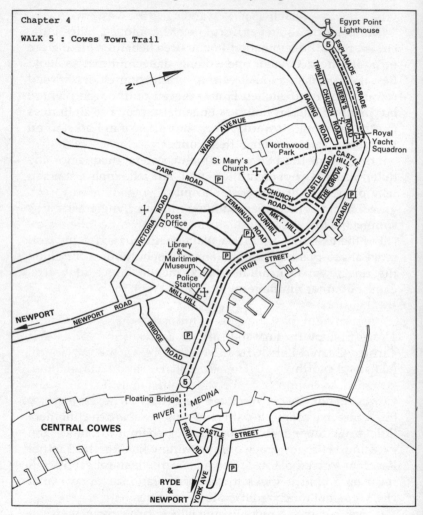

Samuel White's famous yard warships were built for the
Royal Navy, the reason for serious air raids during the last
war. Many beautiful models of ships built here and the whole
history of the town can be enjoyed at Cowes Maritime
Museum. Another way to enjoy the story of Cowes is to walk

round the town – allow an hour and a half.

Our town trail starts at Egypt Point lighthouse. During the last war an anti-submarine boom stretched from here right across to the mainland, opened only at secret times to allow passage of British and Allied ships. Following Queen's Road towards Cowes, Beaulieu House is seen on the right, where Napoleon III and his Empress Eugénie stayed in 1872. Princes Green, sloping towards the shore, makes a natural grandstand for watching Red Funnel car ferries plying to Southampton, the hydrofoil, small coasters making for the River Medina, hovercraft on trial and the police launch whipping about like a marine sheepdog.

At the end of the Green stands the most famous building in Cowes, the Royal Yacht Squadron, its lower stones all that are left of Henry VIII's original castle. The Royal Yacht Squadron moved into this building in 1858 and soon after were given the row of small cannon outside by the Prince of Wales. Crowds gather by the jetty in Cowes Week for a glimpse of royal visitors.

We turn right, past the gate, uphill across the road and up a flight of steps through the ornate gateway to Northwood Park. In the midst of lawns and mature trees stands a classical mansion, Northwood House, pillared and pedimented, designed by John Nash for the Ward family in 1837. The grand balls of Cowes Week are held here. From the front of the house we follow a path down to the mother church of Cowes, St Mary's, its square tower again by John Nash. Outside stands the grave of John Sutton, killed in 1815 in the last duel to take place in Cowes. Nearby stands a shattered pillar on a plinth. The war memorial originally stood in the High Street; it was broken during one of the many air raids on the town and re-erected here as a double reminder of wars.

We leave the church past another lodge to the big house down Church Park, turn left, then right down Bar's Hill into Bath Road, and on towards the Parade, a big square open to the sea, the heart of Cowes. On the shelter is a plaque commemorating the sailing of the *Ark* and the *Dove* in 1635 to establish the colony of Maryland. We walk along to the east end and turn up narrow Watch House Lane, home of HM Customs, then left along the narrow High Street to the arched entrance of the Fountain Pier, where a short arcade leads to the pontoon. From here you can look along the waterfront and see marinas, boatyards and private jetties, Red Funnel steamers and Shearwater hydrofoils leaving for Southampton.

Moving on eastward, look out for Beken's in Birmingham Road: the window is always full of the wonderful action sailing photographs which have made the name known all over the world. Further along, on the other side of the road, Westbourne House bears a plaque since it was the home of Thomas Arnold, the famous nineteenth-century headmaster of Rugby School. Continuing east down Medina Road, we enter the most industrial area of the town, passing sailmakers and boatyards to reach the bank of the River Medina. Opposite, the enormous doors of British Hovercraft are painted as a Union Jack: this was originally done for the Queen's Jubilee and was retained by popular request. The way ahead is by the 'floating bridge', a chain ferry crossing the river mouth to East Cowes with views up river along the waterfront and north to the Solent.

Walk 6: Robin Hill
Time: Allow 2 hours
Map: *see* p.99

Robin Hill is a country park three miles out of Newport on the road to Brading, opened some twenty years ago on a south-easterly slope of the downs. A walk round the grounds (admission charge) is full of delightful surprises.

Starting from the café terrace overlooking a long green slope, we turn left past pens of raccoons and servals to a big woodland cage full of enchanting squirrel monkeys, swinging from tree to tree, chasing and grooming – the size of kittens but with longer tails and with thick yellow-and-black fur. Beyond lie the terrapin pool and tortoise garden. We go through double gates into the highest corner of the park, with a view right across the Solent to mainland hills. Across a fence, ostriches and snooty-looking llamas occupy a field, but the chief attraction of Robin Hill is being able to walk about among free-range animals.

In this paddock there is a herd of fallow deer, several bucks with fine antlers, with their does, all of whom had fauns in 1987; in summer they have beautiful coats of dappled chestnut. Naturally extremely shy, they will let you come right among them or share a rest on their sunny slope. There are also Jacob's sheep, goats and ducks wandering about.

Turning downhill, be careful of the little heaps of earth thrown up here and there. Each is the entrance to a vast underground burrow excavated by prairie marmots from Mexico, which pop up under your feet, sitting bolt upright like oversized guinea-pigs and barking – hence their nickname, prairie dogs.

Towards the bottom of the slope, double gates give onto another section, half grass, half woodland, uneven underfoot, for beneath lies a Roman villa – at least, its ground floor. This was excavated partially when the park first opened, revealing shapes of rooms and a bath house, but it is re-covered at the moment to preserve it.

Above ground, grazing placidly in the woods, are the wallabies, big, dark eyes eyeing you mildly from their delicate, narrow faces or leaping away to a greener patch, often with the tiny triangular face of a 'joey' peering out from the pouch – a lovely experience wandering among these gentle creatures.

More gates lead to a lake well stocked with tench, perch and carp. Seats by the water invite a rest among many kinds of duck and various geese parading the banks. A bridge to the right leads along the last side of the park through a long avenue of tall pines planted in 1905, drifted with daffodils and later bluebells. The lower woods shelter a pretty water-garden, many pools and streams connected by a maze of paths and little rustic footbridges, with lush water plants, weeping willows and seats here and there. This area of the park is being made suitable for prams and wheelchairs.

The last climb through the pines – a good place to see red squirrels – brings us back to the café terrace, where peacocks walk over your feet and shake out their magnificent tails at courting time.

There are, of course, many other attractions, including an assault course for the really energetic.

V Carisbrooke and Central Wight

Walk 1: Carisbrooke to Castle circular
Distance: 1 mile (1.6 kilometres)
Map: *see* p.112

Map: *see* p.112

Carisbrooke village street winds uphill through the valley between St Mary's, the great Norman church on its mound to the north, and the high keep of the castle to the south, a village so steeped in history that it deserves a walk to itself. The High Street offers antique and craft shops, an Italian restaurant and a fish restaurant selling local crabs and lobsters in their season.

We turn right out of the central car-park, or from the bus stop beside it, down the street past the Eight Bells pub into Spring Lane, beside the stream, where the old waterworks building stands on the site of Priory Mill. Though this has long gone, its millpond remains, recently opened to the public. Seats by the water make a pleasant picnic spot, where we may likely be joined by mallard and muscovy ducks. At the top of Spring Lane we cross the road onto a sunken path, locally called 'The Shrubbery', though actually it leads under huge old beech trees.

We turn right at the top along a short lane which leads out onto the grassy 'moats' of Carisbrooke Castle, the inner banks topped by stone walls beyond which high, steep slopes lead up to the curtain walls. The keep is higher still.

The moats along the back of the castle have a view of the western downs, and nearer at hand unusual wild flowers

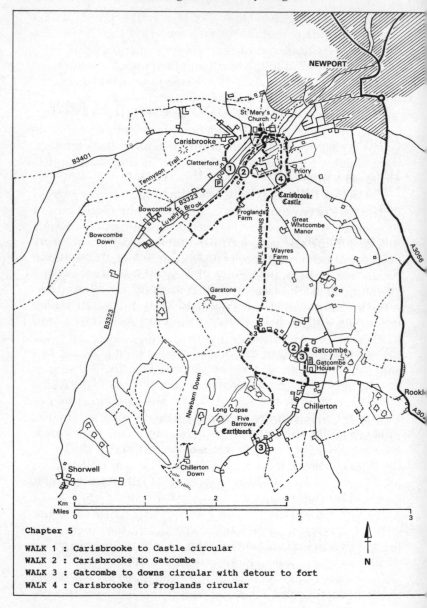

Chapter 5

WALK 1 : Carisbrooke to Castle circular
WALK 2 : Carisbrooke to Gatcombe
WALK 3 : Gatcombe to downs circular with detour to fort
WALK 4 : Carisbrooke to Froglands circular

such as viper's bugloss with its sky-blue spikes, green alkanet and three kinds of orchid. At dusk the visitors go home and the little owls come out of their roosts in the old walls. The moat swings round to the north and the famous drumtowers of the castle entrance – there is a charge to go inside them, but the moats are free – past this the grass begins again.

From this north side the whole of Carisbrooke is spread below, the Lukely Brook widening into millponds in its valley. A seat overlooks it all. From the high walls behind us, King Charles I looked out at this view, as did his daughter Elizabeth, a little later.

Just beyond the seat, steps lead down to the road. Across this a lane curves round into Castle Street, the oldest part of the village, which used to be lined with tea-gardens. Kent's Mill beside the stream which runs by the lane, has recently been saved from ruin, and its pond cleaned out. Castle Street comes out right opposite the church and a climb up the Wedding Steps. St Mary's was built by Benedictine monks to serve the priory which once stood to the north. Walk round it to find old walls and a farmhouse built of priory stones after its dissolution. From the churchyard a meadow path leads toward Newport, and steps lead down to the street and car-park.

Walk 2: Carisbrooke to Gatcombe
Distance: 2½ miles (4 kilometres)
Map: *see* p.112

Apart from its own interest, Carisbrooke is a good centre to walk from. The Tennyson Trail begins here, described on pp.42-6.

Our next walk is to the village of Gatcombe. This time we go down Castle Street but, where it swings round by the end of the stream, carry straight on along narrow Millers Lane with glimpses of the stream and millpond, much distant quacking and sheets of marsh marigolds in early spring.

Where the lane meets another, a steep chalk track on the left leads up to the castle, while to the right the lane comes to a ford and footbridge over the Lukely Brook, with a footpath beside it leading through marshy meadows to Bowcombe valley, good for wet-loving plants such as lady's smock but obliging walkers to wear boots in all seasons.

We carry straight on along a gravelled lane, over a stream to a T-junction, and take the left hand with a view of the south side of the castle, until almost at the road, where a path branches off right, signposted to Gatcombe along Dark Lane.

The first few yards are open field, with a wide view across central Wight, but soon the lane becomes dark – indeed, sunken between deep banks surmounted by tall hazels which roof over the path so we walk in a green gloom even on a bright day. Ferns flourish in the banks, with primroses, wild arum and drapes of moss. Wrens set up their scolding alarm cries, as they have for thousands of years, for this is reckoned one of the oldest island tracks. Under foot it is rough going: after a heavy downpour it becomes a watercourse, so the sandy floor is littered with large stones.

After a long, gradual climb in this green tunnel, it is a relief to burst out into the open. From the field you can see the Solent and Medina valley in the north, right round towards the vale of Arreton and far circling downs. The nearer ones seem less high now we are standing near the 100 foot contour. A good wide track keeps along by the hedge, appearing to aim at the TV mast on the down ahead, then dips down into a bracken hollow where a path goes down to the left. This leads down past a farm to the Whitcombe road. We keep straight, climbing up from the hollow and over a gate. (Most of the gates on this walk have to be climbed.) The path leads on, with a curious field boundary alongside, a small cliff ten to twelve feet high, eroded into ridges and hollows, topped by wind-wizened ash and thorn – an old quarry.

The next gate leads to a short stretch of straight track, then a T-junction. We take the left hand through a field sloping away to woods. Once past these, we can look down into Gatcombe, the top of the church tower just poking up through trees. Ducking under a bar, we reach a narrow tarmac lane and follow this straight on past the farm to the main road, where we turn right, down steep Doctor's Lane, past the rectory. The old road from Newport once led up past Hill Farm, then turned downhill at an angle straight to the church – you can still see a line of trees marking the route – but when a certain Dr Lowe become squire, he disliked having his park tramped across and so made the detour, Doctor's Shute, which brings us into the village street, where we turn left to reach St Olave's.

Though only three miles from Newport, Gatcombe has a remote, secret air, for tucked in a deep fold its narrow road peters out into lanes leading only deeper into the country – like Newtown, it is not on the way to anywhere, a good centre for simply rambling about its maze of lanes and tracks. The thirteenth-century church is full of interest: an ancient wooden effigy thought to be a Crusader's tomb, early stained glass depicting curious golden angels all feathered, mouthing gargoyles and the legend of a little ghost dog who on nights of full moon 'goes forth joyously and dances on his hind legs'.

Walk 3: Gatcombe and the downs circular, with detour to fort
Distance: 2 miles (3.2 kilometres) or 3½ miles (5.6 kilometres) with detour to fort
Map: *see* p.112

A circular walk starts at Gatcombe's church gate, where there is room to park. Turn up the steep track through tall oaks, sycamores and clumps of fern. At the top this becomes a narrow path with a tall hedge on one side and glimpses of the downs beyond. The main stretch is dead straight, because this was originally a church path, the quickest way on foot from Chillerton, which has no church of its own, to St Olave's. Coming out into the open suddenly, there is a wide view of central Wight, undulating away to the far southern hills in a patchwork of copse and many-coloured fields. Three bends bring cottages into view and a crossroad of paths. Straight on leads across the stream into Chillerton village, but we take the right-hand turn signposted to Newbarn, a white track climbing slowly between rolling fields and a very tall thorn hedge.

In summer the banks are real flower-gardens, with lovely massed displays of colour: chalk-loving scabious, purple knapweeds, yellow St John's wort and spikes of agrimony, with sweet-smelling herbs such as thyme, basil and marjoram. At the top of the rise, look back for unexpected glimpses of Culver Cliff far to the south-east. The field falls away and what appears to be the heavily wooded slopes of a round hill begins to loom ahead. It is called Tolt and is really a spur of the great ridge of Chillerton Down. At the end of the field the way back leads through a gate, but a detour left climbs to the island's only Iron Age fort, winding up through huge old ash trees and beeches till a gate leads out onto the bare summit. There on the left are conspicuous raised turf banks – avoid them: it is Chillerton Reservoir! Walk south along the flat ridge till a long hummock roughly shaped in five hillocks comes into sight, very unimpressive to anyone who has seen Maiden Castle, for example, and apparently never finished, but worth visiting for the summit walk and panoramic view of south Wight spreading away to the English Channel.

Retracing our steps to the foot of Tolt, wood pigeons croo-crooing peacefully from the beeches, we turn through the gate and find another hidden valley, fields sloping gently away to steeply rising downland with an enticing white path sloping up its side. Our track continues down the side of the field to a gate at the corner and out onto a narrow tarmac lane. (Bear left up the drive of Newbarn Farm if you want to climb Garstons Down behind.) Ash and hazel on high banks lean over to form a green tunnel. At a T-junction the left-hand sunken lane continues on to a farm from which another downland path begins, and finally reaches the Newport to Shorwell road. We turn right along Gatcombe's 'main street' – so far as it has one, a straggle of stone cottages.

A memorial seat just beyond the junction looks up towards rising ground and a small group of buildings which house the Isle of Wight foxhounds. A footpath to Carisbrooke climbs this bank and goes right past. Make a small detour if you want to be inspected by dozens of wet black noses through the fence, otherwise the lane leads back through the bottom of the valley to a clump of huge old beeches and the church. You can follow the lane on round to the Newport to Chale road where there are buses.

Walk 4: Carisbrooke to Froglands circular
Distance: 2½ miles (4 kilometres)
Map: *see* p.112

A circular walk from Carisbrooke begins at the viewpoint car-park on the road to Chillerton, opposite St Dominic's Priory.

From the village, take the route described in the first walk up Spring Lane and The Shrubbery. At the top, walk left onto the road, reaching the car-park in 200 yards. Walk a short distance along the road, turning off at the corner onto a rough lane, ignoring the left turn to Gatcombe, with a fine view of the south side of Carisbrooke Castle and the keep high above. At a junction, keep left and pass Froglands Farm, the lane changing in character now, with deep flowery banks, often muddy past the farm. It wanders on through farmlands till a sharp turn brings us face to face with the steep slope of Bowcombe Down rising straight ahead. Soon after a path to the left, we turn off to the right along a field path and a footbridge over the little Lukely Brook, an area called Plaish, pronounced plash.

Now we keep along by the stream through marshy meadows – for which you probably need boots, winter or summer. This is a delightful stretch, haunt of wild duck and moorhen and bright with yellow irises, marsh marigolds, milkmaids and many other water plants in their season. It ends at stepping-stones and a stile leading out to Clatterford Shute beside a ford. Here there once stood a papermill, the first of many mills turned by this small stream. Though the name does not appear on any map, the older inhabitants of Carisbrooke still call these meadows 'Papermills'.

We turn away from the ford, shortly coming to a crossroads of lanes. Millers Lane on the left would take us back to Castle Street and Carisbrooke Village. We continue on round to the right to another ford and footbridge over a stream rising just beneath the castle. (By tradition this is the purest water on the island, said to be melted snow water flowing underground from Switzerland and said to have cured various sick locals.) This brings us back to the lane where we started, a left turn leading along the lane back to the car-park.

Walk 5: Rookley to Chillerton with an extension to Carisbrooke
Distance: 1½ miles (2.4 kilometres) or 4 miles (6.4 kilometres) if extended to Carisbrooke
Map: *see* p.119

Rookley is three miles south of Carisbrooke. For many years its centre was a brickworks with a tall chimney-stack, said to be the very centre of the island. Today it is a working village strung along the main Newport to Shanklin road with an industrial estate next door to a country park, not a prettied-up place like neighbouring Godshill but a useful walking centre, especially for those using buses, since you can walk to other villages and still pick up a bus back to Newport.

A walk through varied country to Chillerton and Gatcombe begins in the centre of the village, a few yards before the main

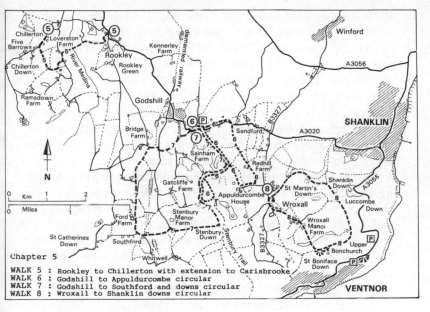

Chapter 5

WALK 5 : Rookley to Chillerton with extension to Carisbrooke
WALK 6 : Godshill to Appuldurcombe circular
WALK 7 : Godshill to Southford and downs circular
WALK 8 : Wroxall to Shanklin downs circular

road forks, up Bunkers Lane, a gravelly track with a few houses tucked away. Ignoring a signpost to Rookley Green, we pass the last house and walk along a straight tree-hung lane leading quickly to a gate into the woods, Bunkers Copse, which slope down to the north, particularly lovely in autumn when the many very tall sweet-chestnut trees turn bright shades of amber.

A good, wide track presently climbs up out of the wood, though still hung with trees. Where farm buildings are glimpsed on the right, it swings round a bend and brings one face to face with a large notice saying 'No Right of Way'. However, our way forward lies over a stile on the left, to the hedge which we follow right down into the valley bottom to climb another stile. We make across a narrow field to a gated footbridge over the infant River Medina, and straight on to another stile. The path tends to vanish here, as there is no hedge to follow. The right of way is still straight ahead, up a hill towards a group of farm buildings called Loverston.

We turn left alone the narrow lane past the farm, with a wide view over central Wight, till it swings round to the west, where we leave it for the drive up to Ramsdown Farm, signposted to Chillerton. Fork right away from the house entrance, then turn quickly between two barns (don't be temped to go on downhill). The farmyard is a favourite hunting-ground for kestrels; in summer you can often hear the shrill, urgent kee-kee cry of young ones squabbling over prey. Where the path swings round, we can see the handsome stone farmhouse, till the going becomes rough and steep, needing all one's attention, climbing between deep banks reminiscent of Devon, but past an old cart shed the path levels out along the top of the ridge to a signpost.

It is worth passing this just a few yards to a gap in the hedge and gateway. On a clear day you can see – if not 'forever' – at least from the mainland beyond the Solent to the white fall of Culver Cliff into Sandown Bay, with all the peaceful, undulating country between them. Returning to the signpost, take the bridle road for Chillerton which swings round to face the long green flank of Chillerton Down, between the fields. Where it turns left, we walk only a few yards before turning downhill to the right into a beautiful sunken path, well named Hollow Lane, banked with bracken. Lower down, the sides are higher still, topped with contorted oak and hazel which lean out from either side interlacing with each other and making a perfect tunnel, though a more spacious one than Dark Lanes. In this cool, dun air, ferns flourish all down the banks.

We emerge onto a wider, open lane where houses begin, beside a little stream which used to be channelled here to provide the village sheepwash, and reach the road beside an old chapel now refurbished as a community centre. There are bus stops here, or we can turn right along Chillerton's main street and walk along the church path previously noted, to Gatcombe and Carisbrooke.

Walk 6: Godshill to Appuldurcombe circular
Distance: 4 miles (6.4 kilometres)
Map: *see* p.119

In summer, Godshill village, two miles beyond Rookley, is all agog with visitors enjoying the souvenir ships, tea-gardens, wishing-well and pretty thatched cottages, but it is also the heart of unspoilt country. A few yards walk away away from the main road, all is peaceful, the only crowds in sight a dozen rabbits grazing or a flock of rooks. As at Brading, a visit to the church will help history and landscape come alive.

Legend, a well-known one, tells how the church was begun in a low-lying field but every night the stones were transported miraculously to the hilltop, so there it stands, high above the village, a fine, spacious building approached by a steep footpath from the village centre. The great house in these parts has always been Appuldurcombe. After its suppression as a priory, it came into the hands of the Leigh family, then for 300 years the Worsleys. Sir Robert pulled down the Elizabethan house and built a classical pillared mansion in its place. All round the church are monuments to the Leighs and Worsleys.

A circular walk including Appuldurcombe begins at the other end of the village. Walk along the street towards Shanklin, passing a picturesque pub, the Griffin, with high Tudor-style chimneys, though actually Victorian; there is a car-park opposite. A little further along, on the right, we turn off through a gate beside a cattle grid, up a long drive between oak copse and undulating green parkland. A bend brings into view a dramatic scarp of down ahead, patched with copse, topped by a pillar. Here the path is mucky from constant passing of cows, but only for a hundred yards or so.

A signpost points right to Sainham, a meadow path which brings you out towards the Godshill to Whitwell road. We keep straight on through a gate onto a broad track climbing up through the fields – imagine what a long pull it used to be for horses, for, though Appuldurcombe is actually in Wroxall village, we are walking up its main drive. At the top of the rise a valley opens out below full of silvery willows, with a wood of tall old chestnut and beech on the other side. But straight ahead – on the very crest and a true surprise in this homely rural landscape – the path is spanned by an ornate, triple-arched gateway, the Freemantle Gate.

Before passing through, we can make a detour to see that monument on the skyline. Signposted to Stenbury and Sainham, a path goes through a gate, up through the woods to the foot of the down which here drops in a sheer wall of broken rock called Gat Cliff. A scramble up round the side of this, on grass 'steps', brings us quickly to a false summit, a hollow with a few ash trees and splendid views, a good picnic spot. A short climb further and the summit is reached. The monument of Cornish granite was put up by Sir Richard Worsley in memory of Sir Robert, but it has been struck by lightning and variously damaged – what one really climbs for is the view, the whole southern half of the island laid out like a map below, from the Needles in the west to Bembridge harbour in the east.

Returning to the Freemantle Gate, we pass through the smaller right-hand one – the wrought iron is very heavy, the central span being of course for carriages. Beside it lie the ruins of the gatekeeper's cottage. The path carries on a short way beside the fence, then swerves off to the left across a field and downhill to a gate onto a gravelled drive, with a view of Wroxall ahead in its fold of the hills. Past a stone farmhouse the road curves round past the entrance to Appuldurcombe, open all the year round.

After the Worsleys left, the house was used as a school, to billet troops and, once more, to house monks, for a brief period while the new Quarr Abbey was being built, but a landmine during the last war left it an echoing ruin. The carved and pillared front is still magnificent, and the grounds, laid out by 'Capability' Brown, are full of fine old trees and drifted with daffodils in spring.

The drive continues on downhill as a footpath to the

village, between newly planted five-foot horse-chestnuts which will one day form a splendid avenue – half way down on either side are two tall ones of a previous generation. At the car-park, one can go straight on up the hill to Wroxall village or circle back to Godshill turn left along Redhill Lane – tarmac but with little traffic, with a very tall ancient wall alongside. This gives way to high banks topped with hedges rather like a Devon lane, and in spring bright with celandine and stitchwort, campion and parsley. It climbs up towards a group of stone farm buildings up on the bank, with a view of central Wight opening up across meadows.

Here, and elsewhere round Godshill, various footpaths are signposted across fields. While these are green and quiet ways, they can be very muddy after heavy rain in any season and difficult walking even in boots.

Redhill Lane winds along uphill and down, circling round to join the main road at the hamlet of Sandford, where we turn left. This circular route does entail half a mile of walking back along the busy Newport to Shanklin road.

Walk 7: Godshill to Southford and downs circular
Distance: 5 miles (8 kilometres)
Map: *see* p.119

Another walk from Godshill starts from the car-park opposite the Griffin. We take the lane beside the pub, called Hollow Glades, a pretty sunken way between deep fern banks with trees interlacing overhead to form a green shade. This climbs to a T-junction with another lane, where we turn left, then right almost at once, to reach a main road. Crossing almost straight over, we go downhill a short way to a bridge over a stream, the infant River Yar in fact, and turn off the lane where the signpost points upstream. This appears to be the drive of a house called Lower Elliots but, where the drive turns off, the path goes straight ahead to a fence, then swerves right over a little wooden footbridge. The marsh is lush green and bright in summer with comfrey, marsh marigolds and water mint.

The path enters a delightful stretch here, terracing along the foot of a deep hedge bank just above the stream, up and down small steps between campions and bluebells in spring. Over a stile we turn left across another footbridge and, reaching the main stream hung with willows, turn along beside it through several small fields, sometimes ducking or jumping single-strand wire fences, with a farm coming into view ahead and the view opening out to St Catherine's Down beyond. Following the fence round to the farm, three stiles and a small paddock bring us out onto the farm road, where we turn left over the bridge and quickly right into a long meadow, keeping along the top of the bank. In spring this is often full of ewes with their lambs, so keep dogs on leads.

A very high stile brings the path back to the streamside, a rough stretch underfoot though overhung with blackthorn and ash, then over a stile and footbridge to continue along the other bank of the stream, past a small sewage farm tucked away here, to Ford Farm. Coming out onto the farm road, we turn left along it for a short way, then right onto a field path which ambles along by the stream, over another bridge and stile and onto a tarmac lane at Southford, where we turn left for a short distance to meet the road from Godshill to Whitwell.

Cross the road and walk through a farmyard, the old stone buildings of Southford Farm, signposted to Stenbury Farm. A stile leads into a long, narrow butt beside a stream-head for a picturesque ivy-clad archway. This is, in fact, one of the few bridges remaining from the old Newport to Ventnor railway, whose embankment can still be seen beside the road near Southford.

We walk straight on over more stiles and through two more fields, keeping along beside the hedge. To the south the stream comes down through a line of fine old trees, a huge ash and a pollarded willow. Soon the roof of Stenbury comes into sight, a very old name mentioned in Domesday. One of the island's first archaeological finds was made here in 1727 when the moat was being filled in. Ten funerary urns were discovered in the bank, thought to be Bronze Age cremations.

Before reaching the farm, a signpost points to the left for Godshill and the downs. Once over, we turn right and skirt round two corners of the field, a rough and flinty stretch: then a footbridge brings us out onto a farm road leading right to pass the farmhouse and continue on up towards the downs. Through a gate this turns left, terracing along the side flank of the down which rises steeply above, ignoring paths back down into the valley. There are lovely views out across the plain below to the western downs: we are on part of the Stenbury Trail here. Under the dramatic precipice of Gatcliff, we keep round to the right and walk along beneath it, through a wood, to join the track to Appuldurcombe by the Freemantle Gate. Turning left, we walk back to Godshill through the park, previously described in the opposite direction on the previous walk. At the main road, turn left for a short distance to the car-park or bus stop.

Walk 8: Wroxall to Shanklin downs circular
Distance: 5 miles (8 kilometres)
Map: *see* p.119

The highest point on the island is the summit of St Boniface, and the pleasantest route to it is from Wroxall, south of Godshill.

From Wroxall church we walk south along the main road, past cottages built for workmen brought in to excavate the railway tunnel under the down; the church itself is built of stone from that great excavation. Where the road sweeps off to the right, we continue on into Manor Road, past the Star Inn, traffic left behind now, following a narrow lane along a valley beside the overgrown remains of the disused railway track. Past the fine stone farmhouse of Wroxall Cross, the lane crosses a bridge over a track now choked with nettles, passes some cottages and turns uphill into a farmyard, with a long stone barn on the left, across it and into open fields by a signpost. (Disregard various other signposts and tracks leading off.)

The path slopes up to a gate into the woods, home of jays and magpies, where the climb begins in earnest, a stony, narrow way which leads very steeply up through ash and hazel. At the top we turn left where a signpost points to Upper Ventnor and Littelton Down, still climbing between banks of bracken, though not quite so steeply, to a gate onto a narrow tarmac road – and the English Channel spread below, green hills stretching away westward, and to the north the whole island as far as the Solent and the mainland beyond.

A pity the nearer view is blocked by high fences and a radar station with several 'dishes' slowly spinning away. The road runs along the back of this emplacement past old war-time bunkers. We are nearly at 800 feet here, though it seems much higher with the vast plain of the sea glittering far below. You can hear Shanklin church bells if the wind is east.

At the end of the fence, gravel takes over from tarmac as the downland reasserts itself, heather and harebells in bright patches between gorse thickets. At the National Trust sign for Luccombe Down, we go through a gate to begin a splendid long ridge walk – though we are not half way yet, there is no more climbing. This is high lark and pippit country, with a new and vast view opening out eastward. Now we can look down onto Shanklin and beyond to Sandown Bay, across the neck of Culver's white cliffs to yachts sailing out of Bembridge harbour. Here footpaths go off to Shanklin and Ventnor. We keep straight on, through a wicket gate along this horseshoe of downs which slowly curves round toward Wroxall again, bringing St Catherine's Down into view, the Oratory a mere dot at this distance, and nearer, Stenbury with the Worsley Monument for landmark.

The track leads out onto farm land, through several gates: this is St Martin's Down. The Arreton valley comes into view, unmistakable with all its shining glasshouses, though on a dull day they are easily taken for sheets of water. Now the descent begins, bending right, through a gap in the high thorn hedge and then down the rim of a huge grass-grown chalkpit to a wicket gate at the bottom, and a field track leading to a wood. We skirt this for a few yards to the left and find a stile. Keeping to the high path, we are looking down through huge old beeches for a short time before the path leads out into fields again, where we follow the hedge round to its lowest corner.

Before doing that, look across the roofs of Wroxall to the trees on the slope of Stenbury opposite which hide the ruins of Appuldurcombe House. In the heyday of its owners, the Worsleys, a 'medieval' castle was built up here to improve the view from the mansion windows. It had castellated walls, tastefully broken away here and there, which concealed a cottage within – no trace now remains.

Walking down to the field corner, disregard the first stile: the second leads to another field path and a final stile into Castle Road – its name now explained. This brings us over the old railway line again and back into Wroxall, beside the church with its handsome blue clock.

VI   Brighstone and the South-West

Walk 1: Brighstone to downs circular
Distance: 5 miles (8 kilometres)
Map: *see* p.130

Brighstone is three-quarters of a mile from the sea and cliffs, surrounded by hills on two sides and by a maze of lanes on the fourth, one of the very best walking centres for those without transport, because you can set off in any direction and find lovely country from wild shore to sheltered woods. Since the war, the village has increased greatly in size, but most of the new estates are not visible from the village centre, so that it appears 'olde worlde' still, with thatched cottages, pretty gardens and a grey stone church dating from the fourteenth century, associated with three bishops – hence the name of the pub. There are several shops and two tea-gardens.

From the village centre we turn up a short road opposite the Three Bishops, past a pretty and much-photographed row of thatched cottages, North Street, and crossing over Upper Lane, find ourselves in Sandy Lane, a deep, sunken and often muddy path, its high, steep banks home to woodmice and wrens. Local legend says this path was stamped so deep by mammoths long ago coming down off the hills to drink from the stream! This used to be an avenue of tall elms beloved of rooks: you can see some of the stumps remaining, but at the top of the first climb there are more hopeful signs, thickets of young elm which have so far

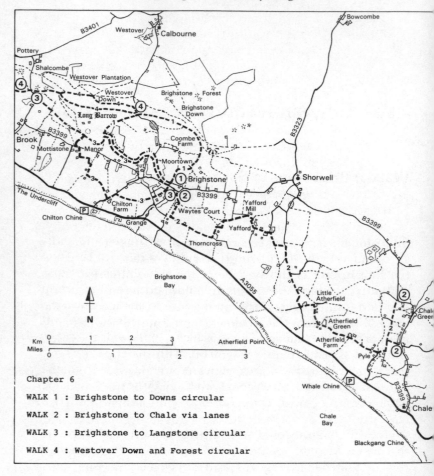

Chapter 6

WALK 1 : Brighstone to Downs circular

WALK 2 : Brighstone to Chale via lanes

WALK 3 : Brighstone to Langstone circular

WALK 4 : Westover Down and Forest circular

escaped the scourge of Dutch elm disease which has so denuded the island landscape, especially here in west Wight, where sea winds make all trees a scarcity.

The path narrows, bears round to the right under a high bank bright with bluebells and campions in spring and soon comes out into the open, rabbit-wide, climbing steeply up through bracken to the summit – and two surprises. Turn round and this short climb rewards you with an incredible view, the whole of the south-west coast, green cliffs and blue Channel. Turn back to the path and you have only reached a false summit – there far ahead and far above lies Brighstone Down, dwarfing this little ridge of Row Down. (Row rhymes with cow and means rough.)

A lane turns off downhill here and would bring you out by a pub called the Countryman on the Shorwell Road; a stile on the other side leads to a path along the top of Row. We walk towards the high down with a hedge on the right and a vast field sloping away into a hidden valley on the left. Presently a lane turns off through this, leading past Combe Farm and out onto the Brighstone to Calbourne Road, but we keep straight on to a fieldgate at the foot of the down, entrance to entirely different terrain: bracken and heather are left behind, for suddenly we are off acid, sandy soil onto chalk.

The path slants up the face of the down, not too steep. Cattle are pastured here, but are mild-natured. A gate at the top gives onto a white track coming over from Shorwell – this really is the summit. Far below, Brighstone village lies amid trees and fields that spread away to the cliffs, eastward to St Catherine's Down and westward to the white cliffs of Freshwater, but the view northward is entirely obscured by plantations of conifers. We turn west along the track, which is very rough in places, with enormous puddles and potholes, past the gate signposted for Carisbrooke, to cross straight over the Calbourne Road into Strawberry Lane.

This is narrow but tarmac, leading down into a valley below Westover Down. At the foot it swerves round toward the sea and, just after we turn off it, over stile, onto a track climbing up through fields to Mottistone Common, a misleading name for a wooded hillside. Another gate brings us into the wood and a wide track terracing along its seaward side through mature Scots pines, a good place for watching red squirrels. A great part of the wood has recently been felled and replanted, though not along the main path. If you want to see this, make a detour over a stile on the left.

Branches from the felled trees (brash) have been left on the ground to shelter new seedlings, so they are quite difficult to see, especially in summer when a wealth of wild flowers springs up to clothe the scarred ground. Take care when walking in hot weather, for adders are common here – also on Row Down.

Back on the main track there are glimpses of the sea before the path suddenly narrows and plunges down a short, steep slope into the woods, floored with a carpet of needles which often show badger scrapings. In winter there are flocks of tits flitting about overhead amid the dark canopy of sea-green needles. At the foot of the hill a stile leads out into a field, with a closer view of Brighstone and the coast. We turn left along the fence to a stile and steps down onto another sunken path, full of foxgloves in June but often muddy. This comes to a T-junction with a gravelled lane where we turn left and almost at once right through a little cut to a stile into a big field. The path is fairly obvious, leading across to a gate uphill on the right; once through this we are corralled between fences for a short distance downhill to a stile leading into the Moors.

Again this is a misleading term, meaning not great stretches of granite hills but copseland growing along a stream. Ignoring a gate to the left, we take the narrow path curving away ahead, sandy or muddy according to weather, through a hazel copse, with glimpses of a stream below. (In spring there are yellow iris and gold marsh marigolds, called 'kingcups' on the island.) This comes out onto a tarmac lane, with houses, for a short space, before turning left, back into the Moors and crossing the stream by a footbridge. Here you can look upstream into a little green world of horsetails and ferns, overhung with alder and oak.

A gentle climb leads into Moortown Lane. Turning downhill for a few hundred yards, we soon come to a footpath up steps on the left which quickly leads into Upper Lane, where we turn right for the village. All along the lower side stretches a field called Blanchards, named after a French family who crossed the Channel on a smuggling trip and, deciding to stay, built a cottage here. (Though her home is long since gone, Madame Blanchard is said to haunt the field.) We are soon back at the foot of Sandy Lane and turn down North Street, to the centre of the village.

Walk 2: Brighstone to Chale via lanes
Distance: 5½ miles (8.8 kilometres)
Map: *see* p.130

Brighstone to Chale is a lane walk, mostly flat with tarmac underfoot all the way, a good winter route when mere paths are muddy and suitable for wheelchair or pushchair. The lanes are narrow, pretty and rural, with little traffic.

We walk eastward along the village street, passing the church and first lane leading towards the sea, to take the second, which leaves the road on a sharp bend. At once the village is left behind: ahead lie only farm, cliff, meadows and the sea. Where the lane bends round to ford a stream, we cross a footbridge and pass the picturesque old farmhouse called Waytes Court, once the hub of Brighstone, for a grander house stood here in the thirteenth century, belonging to the Wayte family who owned most of the village. Here the steward held a court where tenants paid their rents -- hence the name.

At a T-junction we turn left, climbing gently up Wicken Hill, which commands a fine view of the coast right along to the high vertical cliff above Blackgang. A short mast in the field boosts the TV signal for Brighstone. At a small crossroads a lane goes off to the coast on the right; we turn inland past some fine old stone farm buildings, their slate roofs patched with golden lichen, a sign of clean air. The lane curves round through open grassland to a trout farm and a choice of ways.

To reach Yafford Mill by the lane, take the next turning on the right, but we can cut off a corner by taking the footpath to

Yafford, signposted just past the trout farm. This is specially delightful in early spring, when the copse is hazed with green and hung with willow and hazel catkins above banks of primroses; then you can see the chain of natural-looking ponds where the fish are bred, glimpsing coot or mallards. Summer leaves tend to hide them.

The path continues on through paddocks where rare breeds are grazed, so you may get a free sight of, say, Jacob's sheep before regaining the lane opposite Yafford Mill, which was grinding corn till recently; the wheel outside still turns with a great splashing. The mill itself is open in summer, with seals in the millpond, aviaries and a café.

At the next T-junction a turn to the left leads back to the Shorwell road. We turn right and soon come upon a smaller pond, a pretty half moon right by the lane, usually tenanted by ducks and moorhens. Straight on would take us out to the coast. We turn left, under trees for a short distance, then come out into open country, fields spreading away on either side and few hedges, so there is an unimpeded view all round, from the sea to the downs. The lane winds along past a few farms and the hamlet of Atherfield for a couple of miles. Various lanes and tracks turn off inland or seaward; there is a whole maze of lanes between Brighstone and Chale – with a good map, you can make many variations or circular routes or short cuts.

Now a fold of hill looms up ahead, between us and the far green heights of St Catherine's. The lane bends round and changes character to climb Pyle Shute, sunken between high, bare banks overhung with ash and beech, before coming out into the open again. We are almost in Chale, with a choice of routes.

Turn right, downhill to come out in Chale Street, the long road joining Chale Green to Chale village on the coast, where the church stands.

Alternatively keep straight on, climbing slightly for about a mile, which brings us to the outskirts of Chale Green, right beside the Star Inn, where you can get a snack. Notice the high, narrow rear of the pub – this used to be the brewery. Originally beer was made here by one Robert Sprake, from local hops and barley, then distributed round the harvest fields in big barrels. Older inhabitants still refer to the pub as Sprake's Brewery. The road past the pub leads to Chale Green.

Walk 3: Brighstone to Longstone circular
Distance: 4 miles (6.4 kilometres) or 6 miles (9.6 kilometres)
Map: *see* p.130

Returning to Brighstone, we can walk to the Long Stone, then decide on the return route, long or short.

Leave the church and turn up thatch-and-roses North Street to Upper Lane once more, but this time turn left along it, with a view of the downs ahead. At its junction with Moortown Lane we keep straight on up Brighstone Shute, which begins gently but after the last cottages climbs steeply up the downside. Below the road is the Buddle Hole, where a spring issuing out of the chalk gives rise to the stream which flows down through the village and out to sea at Grange. Nearby, on the sheltered southerly slope, a Roman villa has recently been excavated, though it is now re-covered.

Near the top, overgrown chalkpits offer picnic banks with Channel views. On the summit there is an official picnic space for motorists just inside the chalk lane to the right.

We turn down Strawberry Lane once again. There are old lime-kilns here under the down, half overgrown with bramble, splendid for blackberrying, and in summer tiny but delicious wild strawberries grow all along the banks. Down and down, with Westover a high green wall on one side and the lesser, wooded hill of Mottistone Common on the other. Where the lane turns sharply toward the sea, we carry straight on along a track by a small wood, then through a gate into a field, now with woods on the other side, and follow its edge along to a stile. Surprisingly there is a house tucked away up here, originally built for a gamekeeper.

At this knot of paths stands the Long Stone. There are in fact two great stones, one lying prone, the other a tall pillar pitted and grey, though less impressive now against taller trees than when it stood on a bare hillside. All kinds of legends have grown up round the stones: in a summer twilight, with nightjars churring from the woods, you can believe in giants or Druids' rites – actually they are said to be the uprights of a burial chamber, dating from 2000 BC.

If you stand with your back to the keeper's cottage, the track to the left leads down through pine woods to the foot of Strawberry Lane. The path straight ahead is the short way back to Brighstone, and the track on the right the longer way via Brook.

The short way leads down a sunken, dark path under conifers for a short stretch, coming to a T-junction with a wider track. We come straight over this and descend a few steps into a shallow valley of deciduous trees so old that some have fallen and let in the sunlight, known locally as the bluebell woods – come in May and all the ground is hazed with blue. The path descends more steps and becomes sunken between deep banks where wild cherry trees bloom in spring, bringing us to the road at Mottistone, manor, church and a few cottages, all grouped round a little green with a well in the middle.

The fifteenth-century stone church has a roof lined with timbers from the *Cedarine*, wrecked off the beach in 1862. The manor opposite is a fine L-shaped Elizabethan house, still a family home. We walk past it, then turn off down Hoxall Lane, tarmac but very quiet, winding along between primrose banks with a cottage here and there and glimpses of the sea to a wide green space beside Chilton farmhouse. A path on the right leads down to Chilton Chine and the beach.

Here we turn inland, looking up towards the downs till a signpost points off to the right, and we take a field path, called The Packway. This keeps along field edges parallel with the coast till it meets a footpath running from the village to Grange Chine. We turn left for the village, come down into a lane, cross straight over and find ourselves on the recreation ground. Keeping along the hedge to the far side, we cross a footbridge over the Buddle and emerge onto a road of new buildings. Turn right along it a few steps, and a footpath leads up to a kissing-gate and the village school's playing-field. At the top of this we come out into Warne's Lane, which in a few yards brings us back to Brighstone village, just beside the New Inn.

Returning to the Long Stone for the alternative route, we take the right-hand track which terraces along the downside, for a short time bowered in rhododendrons but for the most part through pine woods, with occasional tantalizing glimpses of cliffs and sea far below. The pines are mature, so could be felled at any time, leaving the few beeches fringing the path and revealing the wonderful coastal scenery as it used to be enjoyed before the conifers shut it out, though the red squirrels prefer it this way.

The path leads out onto a drive, the right of way continuing straight down it. The drive itself continues on to Brook Hill, a tall stone house now made into flats, once the home of the author J.B. Priestley. Coming out onto a road, we turn downhill.

You could cross the road and walk on over the downs to Freshwater Bay or turn right for a few yards, then up a track to Westover Down and back to Brighstone. Halfway down the hill Brook church stands on its high bank. Inside hang the Lifeboat memorial boards, detailing the rescues of the Brook boat. In spring the steep churchyard is bright with wild daffodils.

We follow the road down through the village, a straggle of tree-hung cottages, and out onto the Military Road. A gate opposite leads to a rough road and the old lifeboat house. Here a stile marks the cliff path (described in detail on pp.28-30). Keep along the cliff edge with a view south-eastward of all the coast and bays to the heights of St Catherine's and the unmistakable sharp fall of cliff high above Blackgang.

Where the cliffs are broken by Chilton Chine, turn inland along a grass path to a small car-park and the road. Cross straight over, up a gravel track between a scatter of holiday chalets and along a lane leading to Chilton Farm. From here the route is the same as that for the shorter walk.

Walk 4: Westover Down and Forest circular
Distance: 2½ miles (4 kilometres)
Map: *see* p.130

The Jubilee Walk on Westover Down was laid out in 1969 as part of the Forestry Commission's celebrations of its fiftieth anniversary. It starts from the big car-park at the top of Brighstone Shute (on the road to Calbourne).

There are two sets of gates between down and car-park: this is to prevent the straying of sheep, used by the National Trust to keep grass and undergrowth from getting out of hand. We go through the first gate and at once turn north towards the forest, reached through a kissing-gate. In fact, there are three walks: blue waymarks mean one mile, yellow 1¾ miles, and green 2½ miles. Just inside the gate is a maple planted at the opening of the trail in 1969 by Lord Mountbatten, then Governor of the island.

A good, wide track, once gravelled but now largely grass, soon swings round westward, terracing along the hillside just below the summit, with Corsican pines on the higher bank and beech on the lower, falling away quite steeply. Beech and pine were planted in 1950, the pine as nurse trees to the hardwoods. Eventually all the pines will be felled, leaving a beech forest – quite a lot have already been taken out, so this walk is particularly lovely in October when the leaves flame into colour. When we reach the first seat, a blue arrow points uphill through the conifers, the path leading to the bare downs and circling back. We continue on to reach a vast circular clearing, a sort of Piccadilly Circus of the downs, for paths go off in all directions, two back to the Calbourne road, one up to the down and another descending the flank.

We take the left-hand track for a stretch, then, following the yellow arrow, turn uphill along a wide ride between pines and beeches which climbs to a seat and a stile. Once over it, we are on the downland turf and right beside a tumulus, one of a group built on the very highest point in west Wight – indeed, only St Boniface is higher on the whole island. Climb the nearest barrow for a view right out over the western peninsula to the Needles and across the Solent to the New Forest. Near at hand, a tell-tale hollow betrays the sacking of this Bronze Age burial mound, in Victorian times.

Turn eastward and it is downhill over springy turf all the way back (the climb up through the forest is so gradual that you notice only the last few hundred yards). To emphasize the height, we are looking *down* on the Brighstone ridge and its forest, a lovely variegated slope in spring or autumn. Towards the sea, the wooded knoll of Mottistone Common appears to be fringed with pines but bare in the centre, for the newly planted trees are only a foot or two in height.

Close at hand, many small chalk-loving plants abound in the turf, including eyebright, squinancywort, rock rose and the dark blue clustered bellflower, broken up by patches of gorse, bramble and a few solitary wind-pruned thorn trees. The edge of the wood is good bird-watching country, where in summer you may hear the reeling sound of the grasshopper warbler or at night the strange churring of the nightjar; meadow pippits are common, and the whole spread of down is lark country.

Halfway down, a seat invites a pause – it looks out over half the south-western cliffs across Brighstone village to the far southern line of St Catherine's Down, breaking off dramatically above Blackgang. From here it is downhill to the double gates and car-park. If sheep are pastured on the down, dogs must be kept on leads, but they can run free in the forest. Westover Down is part of the Tennyson Trail described on pp.42-6, when it is walked in the opposite direction.

Walk 5: Shorwell village manors circular
Distance: 2 miles (3.2 kilometres)
Map: *see* p.140

Tucked in a wooded hollow close under the downs, with a maze of lanes leading out towards the sea, Shorwell is another good walking centre. A picture-book village full of thatched cottages and ancient manors, it has eschewed the tourist trade – not a tea-garden to be seen, only the small shop-cum-post office and a pub with a stream-side garden. It is also short of parking space, both small car-parks being on the outskirts. These two walks begin from the very small one half way down the steep shute, if coming from Newport, just before a rustic bridge spans the gorge (be careful not to turn into a working quarry, right next door).

The first is a village, lane and downs walk, passing three

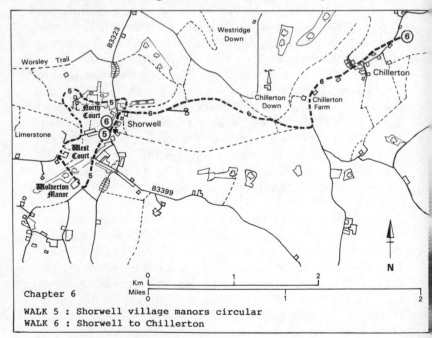

Chapter 6

WALK 5 : Shorwell village manors circular
WALK 6 : Shorwell to Chillerton

manor houses in its circuit.

A few steps down Shorwell Shute from the car-park, a track leads up into a wood of chestnut and sycamore. Keeping to a wide path which swerves round to the left, we soon come to a stile into a small field with glimpses of cottage roofs below and, keeping straight down the slope, reach a gate into a narrow path between gardens – such paths are known as 'snickets'. This comes out into the village street by a row of thatched cottages. (You could start off here from the bus stop.)

Passing the shop, we soon come to St Peter's Church, grey stone with a small spire, its first stones laid in 1100. Pillars still divide it into three chapels, one for each manor, with a fine effigy of Sir John Leigh of North Court in his, but it is also famous for a well-preserved wall painting showing scenes from the life of St Christopher which, though necessarily restored, dates from 1440.

The Crown Inn stands on the opposite corner. We take the road past the church and almost at once turn right down Fine Lane, narrow and pretty, past the old schoolhouse and a mixture of houses old and new, to picturesque Poplyng's Mill, dated 1864, where a short track leads into a very green field – a stream begins right by the path fringed with water mint, rushes and willowherbs. Through the next gate we round some trees and come upon Woolverton Manor, a perfect E-shape with three-storeyed gables, for it was built in Queen Elizabeth's reign by John Dingley, Deputy Governor of the island, on the site of an older house, built by the de Wolvertons and haunted, it is said, by a ghostly minstrel.

A stile leads into a lane, and a footpath turns off at once down the manor drive, through a farmyard and past a huge old stone barn and a very small one perched on staddle stones. We follow the manor wall till it turns a corner – and here it is easy to lose the path. Continue a few steps along the wall till the corner of a cottage juts out. Opposite, a very small plank bridge crosses a ditch on the left and the path turns along the ditchside for a few steps – this can all get grown over very quickly with marsh plants in the summer. Once the path turns into the wood, it is easy to follow, lately widened and made up with stones, a charming little stretch with plank bridges over several streams winding about between yellow iris, ferns and honeysuckle under oak and hazel – Troopers Copse, again said to be haunted, this time by a soldier on horseback who disappeared into it and was never seen again.

A final footbridge into a small field with a gate opposite leads into a white track past farm buildings and Westcourt Manor, also largely Elizabethan but L-shaped and homely among its barns, less grand than Woolverton. At the road we turn right, round a bend, downhill, and look for a signpost on the left between two cottages. Another 'snicket' brings us over a stile onto the downs. In spite of a signpost with two arms, no path is apparent. Strike up the steep slope veering towards a hedge and meet up with an old track now grassy and disused, its course marked by bramble and ragwort: this leads up to a metal gate. Pause here and look round, for the short climb has brought all the coastal plain into view, fields, copse and lanes stretching away to cliffs and sea and the height of St Catherine's.

The gate brings a different view, a valley between the downs. A short stretch of field leads to a stile in the corner and a wood of huge old lime trees, gorgeously scented in spring and a-hum with insects on the blossom. An old kissing-gate is private, leading into North Court grounds only, so we turn left there, down through the wood and over a stile into a field, the estate wall towering above the path, home to mosses, small ferns and ivy-leaved toadflax. Keeping along it, we come to a possibly nettle-grown corner where a stile gives onto a farm track. Westward the farm stands tucked away in this green valley, its land sheltered on all sides by windbreaks of woods, so one of its crops is soft fruit. Through the season it offers self-pick raspberries, currants and strawberries.

We turn away from the farm through rolling parkland undulating up to the downs, dotted with clumps of huge old beech and horse-chestnut, to find North Court Manor, built by the Leigh family in 1615, a tall, many-gabled and rather forbidding house but with beautiful and lovingly tended gardens, where the village Midsummer Fair is held every year. Young Algernon Swinburne used to visit North Court to see his beloved cousin, Mary Gordon.

Just before the farm track leads out into the road, we cross a stile into a wood, and a short steep climb brings us to the rim of the Dell. Long ago a quarry, this huge hollow has long been clothed with sycamore and chestnut, its floor green with ivy and a massed display of shining hart's tongue ferns. In spring it is a sea of garlic – said to be smelt in Carisbrooke when the wind is south-west! In the middle of the Dell stands a footpath map showing various routes that converge here. To reach the car-park we can cross the road straight ahead or climb up to the right and go across the rustic footbridge that spans the Shute.

Walk 6: Shorwell to Chillerton
Distance: 2 miles (3.2 kilometres)
Map: *see* p.140

Map: *see* p.140

The way to Chillerton leaves the car-park at Shorwell by the same route as before (*see* Walk 5), up through the wood and down past the cottages, but here we turn left past a few houses, then out along a farm track, very rough here, with a wooded flank of down on one side, a huge field on the other, gently climbing to the skyline. As the track nears the farm, it is concreted, so easier on the feet, but just before entering the farm itself, turn left through a gate, signposted to Chillerton, and follow the hedge up a steep field to another gate. Here turn across the middle of a big, sloping meadow behind the farm to a signpost on the opposite side, climb a steep bank, go through a small gate and along a fence to a field gate, all splendid cowslip country.

The path now skirts along the bottom of several

long-overgrown chalkpits, often heavily trampled by cattle, with the ITV mast towering above on the height of Chillerton Down. The further pit has various sheltered, seaward-facing hollows for sunny picnics. A fieldgate leads into a deep, high-banked lane coming out onto the main Newport to Chale road near the top of Berry Shute. Turn left downhill to Chillerton village.

Walk 7: Brook to Hamstead
Distance: 8½ miles (13.6 kilometres)
Map: *see* p.145

This next walk, called the Hamstead Trail, has a real island feel to it, since it begins on the wild English Channel coast and ends at a sheltered creek of the Solent, passing through a great variety of country, woods, downs, fields and villages on the way, with the barest minimum of tarmac. A few stretches, churned by cattle hooves, are a bit rough, but stout walking-shoes should be adequate except in winter. This is a good family walk for those with older children, since there is constant change of scenery.

A bus from Newport stops at Brook. At the other end a bus plies from Yarmouth to Newport. The car-park for Brook is a National Trust one, on the cliffs.

Turn right out of the car-park for a few yards along the Military Road, then left to Brook village, facing the range of downs wooded to the east, bare to the west which we are going to cross. On the left stands Hanover House, still roofed by some ancient tiles, now a restaurant with an Egon Ronay recommendation. Round a bend the village comes into view, a straggle of cottages in pretty gardens facing a small green, but our route turns left here, signposted 'Bridleway to Brook Down', opposite a farmyard.

Passing pretty Badgers Cottage, the lane dwindles almost at once into a footpath between very high hedges, some of them elm. Perhaps these also will grow on to replace the

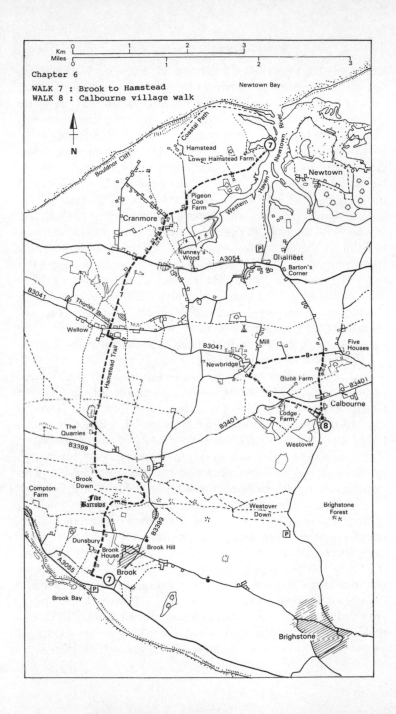

Km
Miles

Chapter 6

WALK 7 : Brook to Hamstead
WALK 8 : Calbourne village walk

N

Newtown Bay

Bouldnor Cliff

Coastal Path

Hamstead
Lower Hamstead Farm

Newtown River

Newtown

Pigeon
Coo
Farm

Western Haven

Cranmore

Nunney's
Wood

A3054

P

Shalfleet

Barton's
Corner

B3041

Thorley Brook

Wellow

B3041

Mill

Five
Houses

Newbridge

8

Glebe Farm

B3401

8

Calbourne

Lodge
Farm

Westover

B3401

The
Quarries

B3399

Brook
Down

Compton
Farm

Five Barrows

Westover
Down

Brighstone
Forest

Dunsbury

B3399

Brook Hill

P

A3055

Brook
House

Brook

7

Brook Bay

Brighstone

thousands of trees lost on the island. Curving to the right, one hedge falls away to reveal Brook Down straight ahead, with its Five Barrows silhouetted against the sky. A grass track gives off to the left through the fields, signposted to the Coastguard Cottages – this makes a short circular walk back to Brook village, but our path lies straight ahead, with a wood called Bush Rew to one side and a wide spread of green fields to the left, blue sea and white cliffs beyond. This comes out onto a farm road with a view right to Brook Hill House.

The signpost to the left marks a track leading back to the Military Road and Shippards Chine. This makes another circular walk, returning to Brook along the shore, tide permitting, or over the cliffs. Our path lies straight across the farm road, with Dunsbury Farm below, tucked into a fold of the downs. This walk is a very pretty and easy way to reach the downs from the coast – the actual road is steep and shut-in by comparison. The lane becomes sunken now, the steepest climb so far, with tall ferns growing in the banks, overhung with oak trees.

At the T-junction, the lane to the left leads along a lower ridge and through meadows, rich in summer wild flowers, to Compton farmyard, where the farm road to the left leads to the Military Road, making one more possible circular route. Pause here anyway. We seem to burst out of the enclosed lane into a vastness of sea and hills, looking right down into Freshwater Bay, almost enclosed by the great white cliffs beyond, strangely shadow-marked, like the face of the moon. Our route turns right, past a scrubby wood to an iron gate.

Once through this, we are on the downs. There are often cattle pastured here and, though they are mild-tempered, dogs should go on leads. A white track climbing up on the left is part of the Tennyson Trail to the Needles. We keep along the foot of the slope to the right, through a gate into a small car-park – we could have picked up the Hamstead Trail here, shortening it by a mile. A short lane ahead leads out to the main road and eastward over Westover Down, but we take a gravel track on the left, through a fieldgate, which climbs up the shoulder of the hill past a young beech wood, thin trunks so densely planted that the light is dim beneath them even in sunshine. Where the track sweeps round to the left, the flat northern part of the island comes suddenly into view, a patchwork of fields all green and brown – and in summer bright yellow from the rape flowers grown for their seed oil.

Just below the bend, the turfed flat top of a small reservoir makes a pleasant picnic spot; eastward lies the huge wooded flank of Westover Down. Depending on the season, a fine variety of wild flowers brightens the banks: yellow crosswort, bugle, milkworts, willowherbs and coltsfoot the earliest of all. Wood pigeons croo-croo from the beeches. The track heads westward, becoming a green tunnel under ash and willow. Where it curves to the right, we take a much narrower but obviously better-used path which forks left into the wood itself. Should this turning be missed (it is one of the few not signposted), you will come to a dead end a mere 200 yards further on – indeed, it is worth doing this in late spring for the wonderful display of cowslips at the end.

The narrow path winds past scrub oak, wild currant and the giant rhubarb-like leaves of burdock, through a small gate into a field, and turns right, leading downhill along the wood's edge, with a vast view across the island to the Solent and mainland beyond, leaving an old chalkpit on the left, to a fieldgate giving onto the Newport to Freshwater road. Straight across, a signpost points north for the Hamstead Trail.

This carries on between hedges joining a concrete farm road for a hundred yards, then a lane. Turn left along it and then almost at once right down a white track signposted to Wellow. We are off the chalk now, yet the track is white. In fact, it leads past quarries with limestone outcrops – the keen botanist may like to explore its banks, though take care if bulldozers are working. The lane is walled with cow parsley in June – on the island it has the charming name Lady's Lace. At the end of high thorn hedges we come to fields with a 'Dog on Lead' notice, views of Newtown Creek ahead and a spread of farmland patched here and there with little copses. A grass track leads to a corner of one copse, but pause a moment to look back at the great line of downs on the southern skyline: already they look gratifyingly far away. A gate leads into a track aiming toward a farm under dark pines. Where it meets a narrow road, turn left and almost at once right, past a white cottage with a lilac hedge. (The post office and general store of scattered Wellow is straight on along the road, just round the bend.)

Passing a few houses and crossing a footbridge over Thorley Brook, we cross another tarmac road and take to the fields again. Cattle use this lane, so it can be very rough, but only for a short stretch. Once over a stile, a green lane leads between high hedges of thorn, wild rose and young elm, through several gates, rising towards a wood – the right-hand hedge dies away but the track can be seen plainly following the line of the left-hand one.

The wood closes round, a little world of its own, the path a green tunnel under oak and ash; where the sun can filter through the canopy, there are glades of bugle and spotted orchids in their season, a very pretty stretch but one of the roughest underfoot, churned up by hooves of cattle and horses, though how they manage the stile at the end, I cannot say. Once over it, into a pasture field, follow along the left-hand fence which leads through oak scrub bordering the field, also rather churned up – plain to see we are on heavy clay. On reaching the road, follow the straggle of copse round to the right where a few yards along two stiles give onto the road, the A3054 Yarmouth to Newport.

We cross this and head north down a potholed gravel road toward the hamlet of Cranmore, in flat, gentle country now. Underfoot the going is very rough for about half a mile, but soon the road noise is left behind, the banks are bright with flowers. We pass a few small houses half hidden in glades, with names such as Sherwood. Turn right at the T-junction past a small, pretty caravan site bowered in birches, called Silver Glades. A notice says 'Road Closed', and a stile by the gate leads into a lane, smoother underfoot and hung over by oak, ash and chestnut, so green and quiet that the loudest sound is a distant cockcrow. A few hundred yards bring us to a white farmhouse on the left, called Pigeon Coo, and almost at once to a narrow private road running north and south, where we turn left and soon right, where a signpost says 'Hamstead Trail, Lower Hamstead 1 mile'.

(You can go straight on – it is very straight, skirting Hamstead Farm and Grange to reach the Solent shore.)

The Hamstead Trail is more varied, first through conifer woods, then oak and ash, with pigeons cooing or clapping their wings the only sound. As the path winds, the trees fall back to reveal the whole range of downs far away along the southern skyline. Round another bend are a first glimpse of shining creekwater and a distant clamour of scolding gulls; further on the Solent itself appears. A footpath goes off to the left signposted to Hamstead, but we keep straight on through flowery banks, especially good in June when wild roses hang their sprays everywhere over purple bush vetch, meadow vetchling, yellow St John's wort and many others.

Passing Creek Farm Cottage on the right and a green farmhouse on the left, we come to – a shop! An unexpected bonus after miles of green ways with hardly a house in sight. It really exists for visiting yachts, stocking everything from white spirit to paperbacks and every sort of grocery. For the walker there are cold drinks, ices, chocolate, even ham and tomatoes if you're hungry.

Having stocked up for a picnic, it is only a few yards down a green tunnel of a lane and here is Newtown Creek, two small jetties leading out to calm waters, boats drawn up on green banks, resident swans, redshank probing the mud, yacht sails and cargo funnels out in the Solent beyond, boats at anchor, bows rippling with water-light, a lovely end to a walk which began on the more dramatic southern coast.

Walk 8: Calbourne village walk
Distance: 1½ miles (2.4 kilometres)
Map: *see* p.145

Calbourne, on the opposite side of Brighstone Down, is a totally unspoiled village with manor, church and mills in a beautiful sunny position facing west. A lane, road and field walk round the village and on to Newbridge can well begin at the church on its mound, one of the oldest foundations in the island, on land granted by King Egbert in 826. From the porch there is a fine view across north-west Wight, and just below the village pump recently restored under a conical roof. Walk along the side of the rectory hedge and down some steps and across the road by a quaint little flint-built lodge. Through the gates you can see a lake with duck nesting-boxes and a drive leading up to a white mansion, eighteenth-century Westover.

Leaving this on the left, we turn down into Winkle Street – or Barrington Row, to give it the old name, a picturesque line of thatched cottages facing a stream bright with mimulus in summer and much photographed by visitors. After the last cottage the lane becomes a path for a short stretch, then leads over the Caul Bourne, which gives the village its name, via a footbridge.

Here the way seems to disappear. Walk up the slope straight ahead and we soon join a path coming across the field at a point midway between two stiles. Turning left, you can see a line of small fields and gates or stiles stretching ahead. These bring us to the farmyard of Fullingmills, the first of five mills once worked by the little Caul Bourne. It is a farm now but was once the place where fleeces, from the vast flocks on the downs, were sent to be washed and rubbed with fuller's earth. The right of way through the farm brings us to the road and a footpath sign right opposite, but it is worth a 300-yard detour along the road to see the next mill, Upper Calbourne, first mentioned in 1229. Now it is open to the public, its complex milling machinery still in place and its millponds transformed into a delightful water-garden with seats by the water and many kinds of duck.

Returning to Fullingmills, we go through a gate opposite and keep along the hedge, ignoring gaps, to a stile. Once over this, turn sharp right and make straight across the field. Sometimes there is a wire fence to follow but it is the kind the farmer moves about. In any case you can soon see a footpath sign pointing towards you, so make for that. A gate leads out onto the road to Newbridge, which we follow downhill to the left for about a quarter of a mile till it takes a right-angled turn uphill.

To see Newbridge itself, walk on up the hill: there is an excellent general store at the top. To walk back to Calbourne, we cross the bottom of the hill, carrying straight on into a lane.

To walk on to Shalfleet, go a few yards up the hill and take the fieldpath signposted on the right. After a few yards the lane forks. To see Lower Calbourne Mill, take the lower lane which soon brings the old stone building in sight below its large pond. Left empty for five years, it was restored to life in 1973 as a bakery and now turns out delicious traditional bread and biscuits in old bread ovens heated by faggots from Brighstone Forest.

Returning to the fork, we take the upper lane, good for primroses and catkins, which winds along to a small crossroads. (Go straight across to explore the farming hamlet of Five Houses.) We turn right along the road and soon reach the larger crossroads with the village straight ahead.

The garage and shop on the corner used to be the industrial hub of the village, turning local timber into wagons sold all over the island. The pub on the opposite corner looks rather modern for Calbourne – in fact, it takes the place of the old thatched one, burned down in 1894, but the 'new' one does bar snacks and hot meals.

VII   Freshwater and the North-West

Walk 1: Freshwater to Yarmouth riverside circular with extension to Compton
Distance: 4 miles (6.4 kilometres) or 6½ miles (10.4 kilometres) with detour
Map: *see* p.154

In 1638 it was proposed that the pebble bank joining the far western peninsula to the main island should be severed, thus creating the Isle of Freshwater – a drawbridge alone would have given access, thus making it easy to defend. Though this never happened, the western triangle *is* called the Isle of Freshwater on old maps, cut off as it was by the wide marshes of the River Yar valley. Freshwater is a red-brick sprawl today, but pleasantly tree-hung, with grassy spaces and streams uniting the old hamlets named from the compass points, Norton, Sutton, Easton, Weston and Middleton, all still to be traced except Sutton, which has become Freshwater Bay.

The nineteenth-century fashion for seaside holidays, Queen Victoria's residence at Osborne, and the Tennyson's arrival at Farringford all contributed to the growth of Freshwater and nearby Totland and Colwell. With the great headland of Tennyson Down, unspoiled coasts and river marshes for contrast, Freshwater makes a splendid centre for the walker.

Our first route penetrates behind the rows of shops to the heart of old Freshwater, the cottages and church above the causeway, where a mill once stood. The church foundation

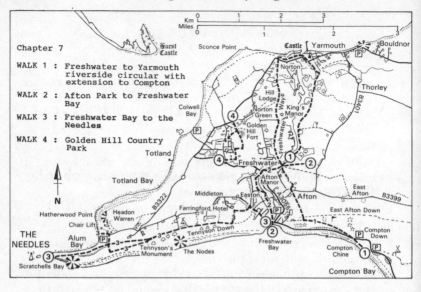

Chapter 7

WALK 1 : Freshwater to Yarmouth riverside circular with extension to Compton

WALK 2 : Afton Park to Freshwater Bay

WALK 3 : Freshwater Bay to the Needles

WALK 4 : Golden Hill Country Park

dates back to the Normans, one of six on the island. To reach it, we start from the roundabout at the foot of Freshwater High Street. The Acorn Spring works stands on the site of the old railway terminus; the marsh footpath starts beside it – you can still see a few lengths of concrete fencing typical of railways.

Soon a stretch of narrow stream comes in sight, the infant River Yar. The path winds along close by it through tall thickets of reed, willowherbs and iris, with duck flying overhead or the loud, abrupt chirrup of coot from the water. Poisonous hemlock grows here, smelling of mice, with purple-spotted stems; as the name implies, this is a freshwater marsh. As with most riverside walks, this stretch can be very muddy – as an alternative, take the path down the opposite bank, which is gravelled, and also leads on to the Causeway.

From the enclosing reeds with occasional river glimpses, we come over a stile onto the Causeway, presented suddenly with a wide shining lake, cottages, a view embracing two church towers, Freshwater up on the left, and Yarmouth far down the river to the north. The Causeway has a sluice beneath, which prevents salt tides flowing any further and dams them back to provide this sheet of water at high tide. We turn left along the road, uphill to All Saints', which is full of reminders of the Tennyson family, including a window designed by G.F. Watts in which the angel has the face of Lady Tennyson.

Our footpath runs beside the wall of the churchyard, a picturesque spread of tombs and marble angels under many different ornamental trees including acacias and maples. A stile leads onto a lane looking down on the river two fields distant. Where this leads into the yard of Freshwater Farm, turn aside to cross a stile and footbridge into a field, often rather rough walking, and follow the hedge round, past another farmyard entrance, to a kissing-gate just past the corner and straight across the drive to Kings Manor, which stands right on the river bank. A wide track leads on towards woods from where you can look across the river to Yarmouth Mill, or back to the line of southern downs from Apse Down in the east, right round to the white walls of Golden Hill Fort, rising above the trees like the superstructure of some great liner.

A path goes off on the left to Norton Green. Our way leads over a stile and footbridge and up along a field hedge, disregarding an inviting wide track to the left. Another field and stile lead to a wood edge particularly pretty in May when the many wild cherry trees are in blossom, and on into an old wood, down between beech, oak and ash all twined and hung with ropes of clematis to a narrow tarmac lane where we turn left past a variety of hedgerow shrubs, wild buddleia, tamarisk and Japanese knotweed to reach the main road. For a splendid picnic spot, cross straight over and round a gate into Southern Water's new amenity, where mown grass banks overlook a whole Solent panorama, Yarmouth harbour, boatyards, church tower and Norton Spit, with the sea beyond.

Walk into Yarmouth over the bridge with a view up the river and take the first turning on the right, following round past the car-park and turning right again by the school. This road leads straight to a footpath along the east bank of the Yar, on a raised causeway passing the old mill, now a private house, to a gate. Once through this, we are on the old railway track from Yarmouth to Freshwater. Sea-lavender, sea-pinks and sea-arrowgrass all thrive along the river bank but the view of this is presently cut off by woodland where, in the shade of oak, ash and hazel, various ferns flourish, including hart's tongue, soft shield and buckler.

A short stretch of open path leads back to the Causeway, once the only highway into west Wight. Cross over and the old railway track continues as a straight gravelled path through the marshes, the river hidden by rushes until a small bridge near the end. Here the path turns a corner and comes out onto the main road. A few yards walk to the right, past the nursery, brings us back to the roundabout at the foot of Freshwater High Street.

Alternatively we could walk an arm of the Freshwater Way which leads over to Compton, on the south-west coast. This detour starts at the Causeway. Instead of crossing the road, turn left and follow it for a short way till it reaches the main road beside the old stone buildings of Afton Farm. Cross over into Manor Road and find a bridleway on the left leading to a gate onto the golf course on Afton Down and a white track. Follow this to the left and climb up to what looks like a large earthwork, across a bank famous for its cowslips. The path swerves round what proves to be a covered reservoir and soon joins the Tennyson Trail coming over from Brook.

From this summit path there is a fine view of Freshwater Bay below and the tall white cliffs beyond, topped by the Tennyson Monument. We cross the Trail, continuing south-east uphill before the path turns downhill across the slope of Compton Down, with a view of contrasting coast now, orange-brown cliffs of no great height scalloped into small, shallow bays stretching away to the height of St

Catherine's Down in the east and the dark, dramatic, broken edge of the cliff above Blackgang. The path follows a little sunken way down to the Military Road, just below a section which is closed from time to time as the cliff erodes ever inland.

We cross the road and join the coastal path along the cliff edge, turning west to Freshwater Bay.

Walk 2: Afton Park to Freshwater Bay
Distance: 1 mile (1.6 kilometres)
Map: *see* p.154

Returning to the roundabout at the foot of Freshwater High Street, another extension of the river walk is to follow the Yar up to its source just below Freshwater Bay.

We cross the road and turn in past a notice saying Afton Park Nature Reserve and are immediately confronted with a choice of ways. Since they circle round, it does not matter which we choose. Both are wide grass paths with occasional seats, overhung with silver birch and willow and fringed with marsh plants such as willowherbs, marsh marigold and yellow iris. Both follow a stream bank where stands of bamboo and reeds give cover for moorhen and mallard, with here and there a waterfall – a very pretty walk, more wooded further on. Where it begins to turn back, a footbridge leads across the stream through a small wood and out onto tarmac Blackbridge Lane. (The bridge is just to the left and worth a few extra steps to lean over and view the stream side and marsh below, for various uncommon plants grow here.)

The walk turns right along a wide grass verge planted with daffodils and shortly turns left onto a narrow gravel path winding through thickets of willows, over small footbridges and through a gate into a fenced stretch snowy with blackthorn blossom in early spring, then over another stile past reedbeds good for bird-watching. This comes out onto a gravel drive where we turn left along a narrow grass way, where a turn to the right brings us quickly into Freshwater Bay.

Walk 3: Freshwater Bay to the Needles, foot of the down
Distance: 3½ miles (5.6 kilometres)
Map: *see* p.154

The route over Tennyson Down from Freshwater Bay to the Needles is described as part of the Tennyson Trail on pp.28-30, but there is an alternative path to be recommended when a strong south-westerly is blowing up the Channel, or for reaching the monument with a less strenuous climb. Follow the road westward past Dimbola flats, once the home of Julia Cameron, the pioneer portrait photographer, who would rush out and seize any passer-by with an interesting face to be posed for her camera. Further on stands St Agnes', the only thatched church on the island, like a beautiful barn. Inside it is full of light from big windows shining on pale stone and wood. There is also a photograph of 'St Agnes' taken by Julia Cameron – it is actually her maid, Margaret.

Just past the church a path turns off through a gate toward the downs. (Room for a few cars on a gravel verge off the road here.) This climbs slowly to a junction with another path coming up along the back wall of Farringford. When Alfred Tennyson and his wife Emily visited the house and saw the marvellous view of downland and coast, they agreed they must buy it. Little Freshwater became the literary focus of England drawing such visitors as Lewis Carroll, Edward Lear and Anthony Trollope.

Just past the lane's junction, a rustic bridge crosses over from Farringford grounds. Here Tennyson would stand of an evening in his black cloak and wide hat, declaiming his verses, to the amazement of the locals.

Our way now follows his favourite path up towards the down, with deep, lush banks on either side, bright with wild flowers and hart's tongue fern, winding through fields to a crossroads, the left-hand path leading back to Freshwater Bay, the narrow steep one straight ahead climbing on up to the summit. We turn right along the foot of the down with a hedge on one side and meadows sloping away, and on the other the downside, here surprisingly covered with trees and scrub.

Look back for a splendid view of Afton Down at an unusual angle and the south-west coast. Here the Poet Laureate used to wander, composing his poems, though there would have been more grazing animals up here to keep down the scrub. The National Trust have reintroduced sheep grazing on some of their properties with this very aim.

The path is splendidly sheltered by downs and hedge. All sorts of chalk-loving plants can be found along it, including yellow wort, cowslips and various orchids. Where the path widens out, a steep scramble round the edge of an old chalkpit would take you up to the Tennyson Monument. Opposite the pit, a lane leads down to the road and Highdown Inn. Hurst Castle is framed between its hedges. Our white track continues past more overgrown pits. In a hedge gap you can look across to Headon Warren and the scar of a sandpit in the valley below, showing where the chalk rock ends. A gentle climb brings us to what appears to be a basket on a pole. This is a half-size replica of the old Nodes Beacon which once stood on the site of Tennyson's cross; beside it stands a stout stump bearing the inscription 'I am all that is left of the Old Nodes Beacon.'

Just beyond, a stile leads out onto the bare down – and surprisingly we are on the summit. Turn back and it is an easy walk of a few hundred yards to the Tennyson Monument. There is the choice of continuing along the ridge to the Needles and Needles Battery or taking the path sloping down to the right. This terraces along the lower downside beside a hedge, turning into a lane on the right which comes out on the Alum Bay road.

Those returning to Freshwater Bay may like to visit

Farringford, now a hotel. Tennyson's study has been retained as he furnished it, together with the visitors' book full of famous names. Pleasant gardens surround the house.

Walk 4: Golden Hill Country Park
Time: Allow 2 hours including a visit to the fort
Map: *see* p.154

Golden Hill Fort tops its small hill like a huge marzipanned cake, a landmark for the whole of west Wight and centre of a stretch of open country. The main entrance is on the left of the Yarmouth to Colwell road and must actually put off some potential visitors as it appears to lead to a factory, but ignore this building on the right and make for the car-park further up the hill. Golden Hill is one of Lord Palmerston's 'follies', built in the mid nineteenth century, like those out in the Solent, in case of invasion from France. It is a huge hexagon with splendid all-round visibility, once defended by eighteen guns. It was also living-quarters for the men who manned the coastal forts below. As a training base, it was in military use right up to 1964.

In the car-park a signpost points four arms. From the right-hand corner a woodland path slopes down a short distance to Heathfield Road, Freshwater. In the opposite direction another short path leads down to the pleasant, tucked-away hamlet of Norton Green, with one shop and a pub. The best walks are round the shoulders of the hill. Leaving the fort entrance on your right, take a track winding gently upwards to an expanse of green turf and a seat, with a suddenly revealed view of downs to the north. As you go downhill, a stretch of the River Yar widens out below, and you see the tower of All Saints' beyond the roofs of Freshwater. Here the track peters out, and you can wander around this southward-facing slope with the chance of sighting yellowhammers flit up from the gorse or the bright wing-flash of a jay.

Turn right across the slope: bushes eventually funnel into a lane running downhill between brakes of thorn and young elm, sometimes becoming a tunnel, a pretty walk in May when violets, campion and hawthorn are in bloom. Small paths lead off here and there for a leisurely exploration (these can be very muddy in winter, impassable without boots). A level, sandy stretch brings you suddenly to a T-junction with a tarmac path and choice of route, west to the centre of the town, east to Freshwater church and the causeway or straight ahead to School Green.

But we have not yet looked at the fort itself, so turn back up the lane, keeping straight on past where we entered it, climbing to a gap in the hedge with another sudden, vast view right across the Solent to the coast of Dorset. As always at Golden Hill, where there is a view, there is a seat to enjoy it: it is a place to wander around rather than to take walks, with a private picnic lawn or a new sea vista to be found round the next gorse thicket. This track leads back to the car-park.

The fort is reached through what seems to be a long tunnel – actually the thickness of its walls; then you are inside the vast hexagonal courtyard with a restaurant on the left and a pub on the right, with tables outside, called, of course, 'The Lord Palmerston'. Part of the fort is given up to light industry, but the rest is honeycombed with craft studios; the barrack rooms all along the first-floor balcony are hung with baskets of geraniums and house – island knitters, soft-toy making, a jewellery workshop, a pottery, leather and copper-work studios, where you can watch various craftsmen at work, or visit the Doll Museum or Camera Museum, an interesting old building put to imaginative modern use.

As the centre of a knot of footpaths, with a large free car-park, Golden Hill is a good starting-point for circular walks. For example, take the route to Freshwater church just described; we can pick up the Freshwater way to Yarmouth and return along the coast turning inland at Fort Albert; there is an entry charge in summer.

Walk 5: Newtown and marshes circular
Distance: 3 miles (4.8 kilometres)
Map: *see* p.163

Newtown, east of Freshwater, is one of the most peaceful green corners of the island, so it is all the more surprising to find a town hall in the middle of it. Nearly 800 years ago the Bishop of Winchester laid out a new town here, a grid of streets on the low-lying banks of a creek which was then a fine harbour. But in the great French raid of 1377 the wooden houses were burned to the ground, and the town never regained its prosperity, even though Queen Elizabeth granted it the right to send two representatives to Parliament.

Today Newtown is a mere scatter of cottages round its church, beside a silted-up creek, but for the walker one of the most interesting places to explore both for its history and for the variety of sea birds out on the salt marshes. There is a car-park opposite the town hall; the only public transport is the post bus. The marsh paths can sometimes be flooded at high tide, so it is best to wear boots against the ensuing mud – and it is not an ideal walk for small children.

The first walk explores the creek and some of the old roads. Turn right out of the car-park into a narrow, flowery lane full of butterflies in summer, passing the town hall. This was once Broad Street, so wide that the town hall stood in the middle of it. Walking downhill, with the chalk hills along the southern sky, we come to Cassey Bridge, a stone arch over an arm of the creek which was once the town's north gate on the route to the bishop's palace at Swainston. Just before the bridge, climb over a stile onto the mudflats, purple with sea-lavender in August. The path leads along beside the creek with a view of masts ahead and always a few blackheaded gulls exploring the mud. Go over two stiles, then turn diagonally across the third meadow to a stile in the far corner and a short stretch of footpath which leads out onto a narrow tarmac lane, actually High Street, with the church opposite.

We keep straight ahead, down the short length of Church

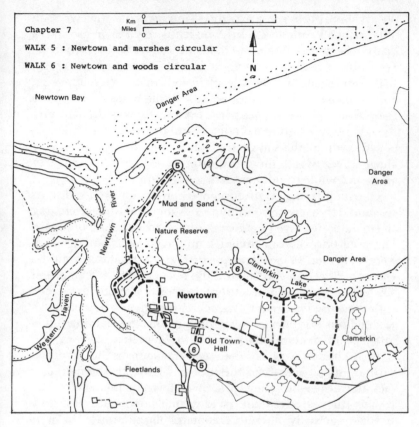

Street before it bends round and becomes Gold Street, a cul-de-sac. At the end, a short stretch of footpath and a swing gate lead to the top of a vast field gently sloping seaward. From the gate there is a view right out over the creek to wooded shore beyond, yachts at anchor, flashing white wings, curlew crying.

The path leads down the hedge, through another swing gate to the saltflats. (On the right a gate leads into the nature reserve, for which you need a permit from the warden's office by the car-park. For serious bird-watchers there are three observation posts.) A long, long and very narrow wooden jetty, with a handrail on one side, leads out to firm ground, a boathouse and seat, and a choice of sea walls. Left from the boathouse a path leads along a green dike and up the creek, with Gull Island a squabble of blackheaded gulls in spring and summer, and on the other side shallow lakes which are the remains of the old saltpans. (Sea-water was drained into these basins and left to evaporate, and the resulting brine was boiled down till the salt crystallized.) The path leads round to Duck Cove, where there are often shelduck to be seen or black-and-white oyster-catchers.

Returning to the boathouse, we can explore the mudflats seaward for a certain distance on the sea wall stretching ahead – the distance depending on its current state of repair. This wall once half-encircled many acres of mudflat which were reclaimed as excellent pasture, but a great storm in the winter of 1954 breached it, and the sea swept in. Ever since, it has been a paradise for waders, herons and gulls: hundreds of Brent geese invade it in winter. Part of the wall towards its east end has been swept away forever, but the National Trust battles with the sea all the time to keep this western end open. Wherever a notice says 'Dangerous to Proceed Further', turn back along the wall and jetty, up the field and back along the lane called Gold Street as far as the bend.

Here carry straight on, over a stile into a long, narrow meadow, actually a continuation of Gold Street. As it is uncultivated, there is a splendid variety of wild flowers and butterflies, and there are blue glimpses of creek through gaps in the high hedge to the north. A stile at the end leads out onto a lane with the town hall and car-park just ahead, passing a large stone house with the seal of Newtown painted on a board above the front door. This was the village pub until 1913: it is known as Noah's Ark from the shape of the boat on the seal.

Walk 6: Newtown and woods circular
Distance: 3 miles (4.8 kilometres)
Map: *see* p.163

The second walk from the car-park at Newtown eventually reaches another arm of the creek but is largely woodland and meadow, flat and easy, though often muddy.

Turn up the green track beside Noah's Ark, once Silver Street, signposted to Porchfield. The space where this widens out is thought to have been the market square. The path turns right through a fenced gap and then left over a stile, and wanders on across a series of long, narrow meadows – just make for the opposite gap in the hedge each time – these are the old strip fields for the villagers. Surrounding oak woods make it a good place for jays, magpies and woodpeckers. An oak copse and two more meadows lead to a stile out onto a lane. A short distance along it to the right brings us to a National Trust sign and a swing gate into Walters Copse, a complete change of scene.

Oak, ash and thorn enclose the path in a green tunnel – sit quiet and you may see red squirrels. Take a turning to the right down a narrower path, then left where it makes a T-junction, a pretty, winding way down to the eastern arm of the creek called Clamerkins, a corruption of the name Glamorgan's, the family which once owned this area.

The waterway is narrow here, with wide banks of spartina grass, sea-pinks, sea-lavender. The path now leads to the left through the grass along the wood's edge, though sometimes entering the wood again to avoid muddy fingers of the creek. In summer there are banks of marshmallow, pale pink flowers with beautiful silvery leaves from which the sweet was originally made; though plentiful here, it is rare over the island, so please do not pick it. The path turns at a right angle into the wood, winds round to a one-plank bridge and emerges on a wider track into Town Copse. A few yards to the right this comes out onto bare mudflats where a seat under an oak tree makes an ideal picnic spot, with a view out over Clamerkins with its black-and-white oyster boats, to the main creek with woods rising inland and to the north the masts and funnels of ships in the Solent.

To find the eastern end of the old sea wall, continue on the path through the edge of the copse, cross the oyster-fishery road, over a stile into a green field called 'The Promised Land'. At the far end, the wall begins but breaks off after only a few yards. Return to the seat. From here a track leads straight up through Town Copse, mostly oak and hazel. Recently the old custom of coppicing has been revived here, harvesting poles from the hazel, which will sprout new ones, for use in fencing and sea defences. This let in more sunlight, and wood anemones sprang up in every clearing. A stile leads out onto a narrow road – Gold Street, in fact. Turn right along it under old oaks and past high hedges until it swings round to the town hall and car-park.

So here in this quiet green corner we come to the end of walking in the Isle of Wight, but only on paper, for we have covered a mere part of that delectable five hundred miles of pathways, enough at least to have sampled the varied scenery and to give the walker appetite for more. The beginnings of various other walks, signposts, and turnings off have been briefly indicated on the way; a good Ordnance Survey map will suggest many others and variants of the walks described here.

The Isle of Wight would like to extend its visitors' season. spring and autumn are ideal for the walker, the landscape full of interest with the year's first flowers or the glowing colours of October. While the deep country is seldom crowded, even in August, approaches to the island can be very busy, whereas in spring and autumn, mainland roads and ferries can be an enjoyable part of the journey. Winter itself is often milder here. Bare-branched woodlands and the wild shores of west Wight hold a special magic in the long shadowed sunlight of December.

Leaflets with notes and maps to accompany each of the seven Long-Distance Trails and the four Coastal Trails are available by post from the County Surveyor, County Hall, Newport, or from Tourist Information Offices (summer only) in Newport, Ryde, Shanklin, Sandown and Yarmouth.

Walks suitable for Prams and Wheelchairs

Firestone Copse (shorter walk)
Ryde Town Trail
Ryde to Seaview
Sandown to Shanklin
Newport Town Trail
Parkhurst Forest (shorter walk)
Gurnard to Cowes
Cowes Town Trail
Robin Hill Woodland Walk

Index

Afton Park Nature Reserve, 157

Albert, Prince, 15, 18

Albion Hotel, 29

Alum Bay, 20, 30

Appuldurcombe, 14, 49, 121-3, 125

Armada, 12

Arreton, 11, 71

Arreton Manor, 12

Ashey Down, 76

Ashey Sea Mark, 40

Atherfield, 134

Barnes High, 27

Barton Manor, 102

Beacon Alley, 48

Bede, the Venerable, 11

Bembridge, 39, 61, 63, 67

Bembridge Trail, 23, 26

Bembridge Windmill, 64

Binstead, 54-5

Bird-watching, 100, 163

Blackgang, 26, 90-4

Blackgang Chine, 92-3

Black Knight rockets, 29

Blacksmiths Arms, 43

Blackwater, 41, 103

Bleakdown, 48

Bonchurch, 19, 79, 82-3

Bowcombe Down, 42

Brading, 10, 11, 63-7

Briddlesford Copse, 17

Brighstone, 27, 43, 46, 49, 129-39

Brighstone Forest, 46

Bronze Age, 10

Brook, 21, 28, 144-6

Brook Down, 10, 43, 146

Brown, 'Capability', 122

Buddle Inn, 88

Cadwalla, 11

Calbourne, 151

Cameron, Julia, 158

Carey, George, 12

Carisbrooke, 10, 12, 13, 17, 20, 22, 26, 42, 102-3, 111-14

Carisbrooke Castle, 17, 111, 113

Castlehaven, 89

Chale, 23, 26, 90-2, 133-5

Charles I, 12, 18, 96

Charles II, 33, 90

Cherbourg, 14
Chillerton, 117, 143-4
Chillerton Down, 10, 118, 120
Chilton Chine, 28, 138
Clamerkins Creek, 36, 165
Clarendon, 91
Coastal Path, 23-38
Colwell, 18, 31
Compton, 153, 156
Compton Down, 21
Cowes, 14, 37-8
Cowes Maritime Museum, 14
Cowes Week, 15
Cranmore, 35, 148
Cubbitt, Thos., 15
Culver, 68

Dark Lanes, 10
Darwin, 18
Davenant, Wm., 17
Dawes, Sophie, 62
de Fortibus, Isabella, 11
de Redvers family, 11
Dickens, C., 83
Dorset, 9
Downland Way, 23, 26, 40, 41, 76

East Cowes, 15, 23, 108
Eastern Yar, 9, 48, 71
Edward, Prince of Wales (Edward VIII), 37
Egypt Point, 107
Eider, 27
Elizabeth I, 12, 162
Enclosure Acts, 13

Farringford, 18, 29, 153, 158, 160
Fielding, H., 15
Firestone Copse, 51-3
Fishbourne, 54
Five Houses, 151
Folly Inn, 98, 102
Forestry Commission, 20, 43, 53, 104, 138
Fort Albert, 32
Fort Redoubt, 29
Fort Victoria, 32
Freshwater, 18, 46, 153-7
Freshwater Bay, 15, 28, 137, 158-9
Freshwater Way, 23, 156

Garibaldi, 18
Gatcombe, 12, 41, 113-17, 118-20
Glanville Fritillary, 21, 22
Godshill, 12, 121-5
Golden Hill Country Park, 160-1
Grange Chine, 27
Gurnard, 10
Gurnard Marsh, 37
Gwilliam, 16

Hampshire, 21
Hants & IOW Naturalists Trust, 21
Hamstead Trail, 23, 35, 144-9
Hanover House, 28
Hanover Point, 28
Hare and Hounds, 41
Headon Hill, 30

Henry VIII, 13, 33, 105
Hildila, 11
Holliers Hotel, 18
Hoy Monument, 91
Hurst Castle, 13

Iron Age, 10
Isle of Wight County Council, 23
Isle of Wight Natural History Society, 21
Isle of Wight Steam Railway, 17

Keats, John, 17-18
Knighton, 74-7

Ladder Chine, 26
Lisle Combe, 19
'Local Look', 21, 22
Locks Heath, 36
London, 29
London Heath, 36
Longfellow, H., 18, 82
Longstone, 135-6
Luccombe, 82-3
Luccombe Down, 126

Marks Corner, 105
Marvel Copse, 102, 103
Medina, River, 9, 11, 98-102
Military Road, 26, 28, 137
Morey, Micah, 41
Mottistone, 135-6
Mottistone Common, 135, 139

Nash, John, 107
National Trust, 29, 64, 83, 126, 138, 144
Nature Conservancy, 21
Needles, the, 20, 22, 29, 30, 39, 159
Needles Battery, 30, 159
Newbridge, 151
Newchurch, 71-4, 77
New Forest, 9
Newport, 13, 20, 22, 26, 95-104
Newtown, 20, 21, 149, 162-6
Newtown Creek, 35
Niton, 14, 86, 88
Nodgham Lane, 18
Norris Castle, 15, 102
Northcourt Manor, 19, 142-3
Norton Green, 160
Norton Spit, 33
Noyes, Alfred, 19, 85
Nunwell House, 12
Nunwell Trail, 23, 26
Nunwell Woods, 39, 66
Nye's Yard, 14

Oglander family, 12, 66
Old Park, 84, 86, 102
Osborne House, 15, 18, 20

Palmerston's Follies, 58, 160
Parkhurst Forest, 104
Porchfield, 36
Puckpool, 58

Quarr Abbey, 11, 54-5, 74

Railways, 16
Ramblers Assoc., 9
Ramsdown Farm, 47, 120
Red Funnel Steamers, 107
Red squirrels, 21, 53
Rew Street, 10
Reynolds, J. Hamilton, 17
Robin Hill Country Park, 108-10
Romans, 10
Rookley, 118
Row Down, 131
Rowridge, 42-3
Royal Yacht Squadron, 107
Ruskin, 18
Ryde, 11, 15, 16, 51, 53, 55-8
    St John's station, 26

Sainham Farm, 48
St Boniface Down, 15, 79, 84
St Catherine's Down, 90, 94
St Catherine's Lighthouse, 89
St Catherine's Oratory, 91
St Dominic's Priory, 104
St Helen's, 61-3
St Lawrence, 19, 86
St Lawrence's Church, 87
St Lawrence's Shute, 87
St Martin's Down, 126
Samphire, 29
Sandown, 15, 67, 69, 71, 77-9
Sandown station, 26
Scotchell's Brook, 72
Seaview, 15, 58-9
Shalfleet, 35, 151
Shanklin, 15, 18, 77-8, 125-6
Shanklin Chine, 79, 82

Shanklin Old Village, 79
Sheepwash Copse, 17
Shepherd's Chine, 26-7
Shepherd's Trail, 23, 26, 27
Shide, 103
Shorwell, 12, 140-5
Sites of Special Scientific Interest, 21
Smugglers Museum, 14, 85
Smuggling, 14
Solent, 15, 16
Southford, 123-4
Spindler, Wm., 85
Steephill Botanic Gardens, 85
Steephill Cove, 84
Stenbury Trail, 23, 49
Stone Age, 10
Sullivan, A., 18
Swinburne, A., 19, 69, 143

Tennyson Down, 29
Tennyson family, 18, 19, 29, 153, 155, 166
Tennyson Trail, 12, 22-3, 26, 42, 113, 139
Thorness, 37
Totland, 15, 18, 31
Town Copse, 165-6
Turf Walk, 31

Undercliff, 9, 11, 15, 19, 84

Ventnor, 14, 15, 47, 84, 86
Victoria, 15, 20, 85

Waders, 33, 164
Walpen Chine, 26

Warden Point, 31
Watcombe Bottom, 49
Watts, G.F., 18
Wellow, 147-8
Westcourt Manor, 141
Westover Down, 43, 46, 131, 137-9
Whale Chine, 27
Wheeler, Robert, 27
Whippingham, 98
Whippingham church, 101-2
Whitecliff Bay, 68
White, John Samuel, 15, 106-7

Wild flowers, 62, 67, 73, 78, 94, 124
Wood calamint, 21
Woolverton Manor, 141
Wootton, 23, 26, 51, 53
Worsley family, 121
Worsley Trail, 23, 46
Wroxall, 121-3, 125, 127

Yafford Mill, 134
Yarborough, Lord, 14
Yarmouth, 13, 153, 161
Yarmouth Castle, 12, 33